ETpedia™

Teenagers

500 ideas for teaching English to teenagers

Edmund Dudley
Series editor: John Hughes

www.myetpedia.com

ENGLISH TEACHING professional

ETpedia

Teenagers

Published by:

Pavilion Publishing and Media Ltd
Rayford House
School Road
Hove BN3 5HX
UK
Tel: 01273 434 943
Fax: 01273 227 308

First published 2018

A catalogue record for this book is available from the British Library.

ISBN: 978-1-911028-44-4

PDF ebook ISBN: 978-1-911028-42-0

Epub ISBN: 978-1-910366-28-8

Kindle ISBN: 978-1-911028-43-7

Author: Edmund Dudley

Editor: Penny Hands

Production editor: Mike Benge, Pavilion Publishing and Media

Cover design: Emma Dawe, Pavilion Publishing and Media

Page layout and typesetting: Anthony Pitt, Pavilion Publishing and Media

Printing: Ashford Press

Contents

Developing skills

Developing language awareness (grammar, vocabulary, pronunciation)

Keeping it real: additional lesson topics and activities

Introduction

10 reasons for using this resource

Introduction

1. **You're new to teaching**
   Less experienced teachers will find this a useful and practical introduction to working with teenage students.

2. **You need some ideas**
   More experienced teachers in search of new ideas will find good, practical activities and techniques here.

3. **You're struggling with teens**
   This book does more than provide classroom ideas: it aims to help teachers better understand teenagers, and to empathise with some of the issues that teenagers have in the classroom.

4. **You've never taught teens before**
   Experienced teachers who are about to work with teenagers for the first time will get a sense of the unique challenge posed by teenage classes.

5. **You read on the run**
   Teachers who need something bite-sized that they can dip into between classes will appreciate the format of the book.

6. **You're looking for staffroom discussion-starters**
   Senior teachers and heads of department can select units of the book to kick-start staffroom conversations, peer collaboration and idea-sharing among colleagues.

7. **You want something that works**
   The ideas in the book are designed to be simple, effective and down-to-earth.

8. **You haven't got much time to prepare lessons**
   Most of the practical ideas and activities in this book are straightforward and need little or no preparation.

9. **You enjoy teaching**
   This book is written for teachers who love teaching, and who want their lessons to be memorable and enjoyable – both for their students and themselves.

10. **You're curious about other teachers' experiences with teens**
    The author has spent many years working with teenagers, thinking about the teenage classroom and discussing teaching with colleagues. The book is a culmination of that process.

10 ways to use this resource

1. **Use it to get ideas when planning lessons**

   This book can be dipped into when planning practical activities for lessons.

2. **Talk about it with your colleagues**

   Read a unit and then discuss it with your colleagues. Share your own ideas and techniques.

3. **See what your teenage students think about it**

   Use one of the units (for example, Unit 4) as reading input in one of your classes. Ask your teenage students if they agree with the views expressed about teenagers.

4. **Read it critically**

   No two teenage classes are the same, and experiences differ. Modify and adapt ideas to suit your own needs.

5. **Add your own ideas in the margins**

   Use this book as a notebook. Jot down your thoughts and new ideas in the margins of each unit.

6. **Read a unit a week**

   Tackle one short unit a week for a manageable and beneficial reading challenge.

7. **Try out one idea every week**

   Choose an idea that you like from each practical unit. Try it out.

8. **Open it at a random page**

   Open the book at random, read one unit, and make a note of one idea to try out, or one view about teenagers to discuss with a colleague.

9. **Compile a 'Top 50'**

   Read the book from cover to cover. At the end of each unit, circle the point that you like the most.

10. **In case of emergency**

    Keep the book in the staffroom for those moments when you need a quick idea for your next lesson.

10 facts about the author

Edmund Dudley ...

- is from the UK, but lives in Budapest.
- started teaching in 1992.
- is a freelance trainer, materials writer and teacher.
- has regular classes with teenage students at PTE Babits Secondary School in Pécs, Hungary.
- also speaks Hungarian – his students' mother tongue – although English is his first language.
- has two daughters, one of them still a teenager. They both agreed to read several units of the first draft of this book, and told their dad which parts were a bit rubbish, which parts weren't that bad, and which parts were cool. He thinks they're the ones who are cool.
- is the co-author (with Erika Osváth) of *Mixed-Ability Teaching*, published by OUP.
- occasionally posts ideas and materials for teachers at legyened.edublogs.org.
- travels a lot and posts pictures on Instagram as edtothemund.
- wasn't always much fun to be around while this book was being written. He is therefore extremely grateful to Sinéad Laffan for her good humour, constant support and expert professional insights, especially about teaching pronunciation and listening. The best ideas in those units are hers.

Preparation and planning

Although there are no hard-and-fast rules about what teenagers are like, teachers who have worked with teens for a long time tend to agree on some of the things that teenagers value in interactions with their teachers – and also on the things that they object to. No such judgements on our part can be completely authoritative – or indeed true for everyone – but this section attempts to list some of these key teen characteristics in the hope that being aware of them can help to make sure that our planning and preparation process is optimised.

One of the distinctive characteristics of the teenage classroom is that you're never quite sure how students are going to react to the materials and activities planned for that day. This can make the task of preparation quite challenging. As teachers, it's important for us to acknowledge – and embrace – that uncertainty. As the units in this section attempt to show, no two teenage groups are the same, and all the individual teenagers in the room are themselves undergoing the significant changes brought on by adolescence. The result is that teenagers often take us by surprise with their responses and reactions to our lessons. Anticipating this beforehand is one step towards being able to deal with it effectively in the classroom.

Careful preparation of language-learning materials is essential of course, as is an attempt to select materials that feel appropriate and interesting. Successful lessons with teenagers sometimes require something beyond appropriate materials, though: teenagers are often looking for a sense that we 'get' them as learners – and as people. The first section of this book, therefore, devotes several units to the important matter of how we can find out about our teenage students. Once we have equipped ourselves with useful information about our students, the materials that we are working with can often be tweaked and tailored to reflect their interests and preferences.

Preparing and planning lessons for teenagers therefore involves looking at both language-teaching considerations and the interpersonal dynamics of the classrooms we work in. As long as we remain flexible in our thinking and open-minded with regard to our students, it is possible to plan lessons that work, and to prepare for classes effectively.

10 ways that teenagers are different from young learners

Adolescence affects students in different ways, so we need to be cautious when drawing conclusions about the ways in which teenage students are different from young learners. Having said that, it is a fact that the teenage years are characterised by the changes brought about by puberty. These changes are not only physical, they also have an effect on the way that students learn, feel and interact with others.

Here are some of the ways that teenagers are different from younger learners.

1. More grown up

Although they are still children in many ways, teenagers are maturing fast and are much more concerned with being treated like adults. In the classroom this means that they reject activities that they deem childish, and are – with some exceptions – generally much less willing to take part in activities that include total physical response, kinaesthetic learning or singing.

2. Longer attention spans

Teenagers have the capacity – though not always the desire – to concentrate for longer periods than young learners. Whereas successful lessons with young learners require huge amounts of variety and regular transitions from activity to activity, lessons with teenagers should be designed partly to nurture this growing capacity they have to sustain concentration for a longer period of time.

3. Better at abstract thinking

Changes to the brain mean that teenagers are better at thinking in abstract terms than young learners. They are also quickly learning to be more analytical and systematic in how they process information about the world. We need to make sure that their growing cognitive capacity is regularly fed with tasks that get them thinking.

4. Body-conscious

The changes to the body that teenagers experience in puberty have a truly significant impact on their lives and the way they see themselves and others. Teenagers are extremely body-conscious – some to the point of distraction – and this makes it hard for them to concentrate in class. As teachers, it is important that we demonstrate sensitivity, understanding and patience, for example by not drawing attention to students' physical appearance.

5. In a world of their own

The egocentrism of adolescence can make many teenagers hard to reach. They can appear distant, distracted, uncommunicative, or just lost in thought. Some teenagers can't seem to stop looking out of the window or at their own reflections. A patient and sensitive attitude from the teacher is the best way to navigate this obstacle. When students' minds have wandered, try to get their attention back in a way that does not make them feel embarrassed or singled out.

6. **Brittle self-confidence**

Although teenagers can appear brash and self-confident, they are far more sensitive to the opinions of others than young learners are, and often regulate their behaviour in order to try to influence what others say about them. Be mindful of the fact that teenagers can be extremely sensitive to offhand comments from their teachers, no matter how bulletproof their behaviour might appear.

7. **More swayed by peer pressure**

Peer pressure is at its highest during the teenage years, when the influence of a pack mentality can sometimes be detected in the decision-making and behaviour of individuals in class. Be aware of this when negotiating with teenagers or discussing issues that affect the whole group: talking to students one-to-one or asking them to write down their opinions individually are the best ways to counter the power of peer pressure and to discover what individuals really think.

8. **Sexually aware**

There is no avoiding the fact that teenagers are growing in sexual maturity and are often pre-occupied with the topic of sex. This can affect how they respond to certain topics and can influence how they conduct themselves in class when working with students they are trying to make an impression on. Teachers of teens need to be calm and assertive when establishing norms of acceptable interaction between students, but should also be understanding of the fact that the inappropriate behaviour of many teens is caused by confusion and insecurity.

9. **More rebellious**

Students tend to become more rebellious as they reach adolescence, a natural consequence of the many changes they are going through on the journey from childhood to adulthood. No longer children, yet not always capable of behaving like adults, teens sometimes see teachers as domineering adult figures who are trying to order them about. In class, this can lead to confrontations and resistance, which are best met with a calm and consistent response. Be willing to hear students out and to compromise where possible. When you stand your ground, do it in a mature and respectful way.

10. **Less concerned with getting the teacher's approval**

Unlike young learners, teenagers care less about what the teacher thinks about them and more about the opinion of their classmates. Telling teenagers you are 'disappointed in them' will not have the same effect as it has on younger learners. Ultimately, teens want to keep some kind of distance between themselves and the teacher, which is quite understandable. Accept it. In the long run, teenagers are actually more likely to warm to teachers who accept them as they are than to those who try to judge them or guilt-trip them.

10 ways that younger teens are different from older teens

At the risk of making generalisations, it's possible to notice a gradual change in teenagers as they get older. Thirteen year olds and 14 year olds tend to conduct themselves in a different way from 18 year olds, and also have a noticeably different attitude towards the learning process.

Teenagers are also developing and maturing at different rates and in different ways, so in many cases we find that there can be a clash of norms within a single group. This is particularly true among 15 year olds and 16 year olds, where developmental differences between individual students can be most marked.

This unit focuses on younger teens, drawing attention to some of the ways in which they are likely to present a slightly different challenge from students a few years older.

1. Noisier

Younger teens are often noisier, more fidgety and more physically energetic in the way they behave in the classroom than older teens. In addition, they are often oblivious to the effect that their behaviour has on others. Be firm and patient when the lively behaviour of younger teens interferes with your teaching, and remember that others in the class are also put off by it. Work hard to establish and enforce ground rules, while also being tolerant of the fact that a certain level of animated behaviour is inevitable at this age.

2. Less self-disciplined

It takes teenagers a few years to develop enough self-discipline to avoid unnecessary conflicts. It can also be hard for them to anticipate the consequences of their actions, and to manage their time effectively. Although problems of this kind are found among teenagers of all ages, it tends to be most acute with younger teens. Instead of just telling them what they're doing is wrong, indicate what steps they can take to put things right.

3. More active and enthusiastic

Younger teenage students often have a strong sense of fun, and bring humour and energy to the classroom. They are often less jaded than older teenage students, who tend to be slightly more serious and goal-oriented. Younger teens want to enjoy themselves in class, and are generally more willing to take part enthusiastically in activities that offer them the chance to do this.

4. More attention-seeking

There are usually more class clowns who are inclined to mess around in order to impress their friends or to try to draw attention to themselves in some way. As they mature, teenagers tend to outgrow the urge to be the centre of attention in lessons, and look for more subtle and sophisticated ways to get the attention and approval of their peers.

5. **Less focused on exams and careers**

Younger teens are generally more concerned with the here-and-now, while the priorities of older teens are more geared towards attaining their goals. As a result, it is difficult to get younger teens to take exam practice seriously, as anything happening in more than a year's time seems to be in the distant future. Older teens, meanwhile, are more concerned with passing their exams, and demand lessons that are more oriented towards helping them practise and prepare.

6. **Less interested in abstract topics**

As they get older, teenage students become more interested in abstract ideas and show greater interest in debating and discussing topics that extend beyond the confines of their own lives. Younger teens have a fast-growing interest in the world at large, but have generally spent less time thinking about abstract topics than their older peers.

7. **Less life experience**

A 14 year old usually has much more limited life experience than someone three or four years older than them, and this lack of experience can have an effect on how well younger teens are able to tackle tasks that draw on real-world situations. Bear this in mind when planning tasks and activities for lessons.

8. **Less sure of themselves**

Younger teens are soaking up the world around them, and as a result are still in the process of forming some of the opinions and values that they will come to have as adults. Older teens generally have a clearer idea of where they stand on certain issues, and so are more self-assured when asked to express opinions, especially on topics connected to the outside world.

9. **More adventurous**

By the time they leave secondary school, many teenagers have fairly pragmatic expectations and ambitions for themselves; younger teens, meanwhile, are more likely to have big dreams. They often have an adventurous, more optimistic outlook on life, which can be harnessed with appropriate tasks in the language classroom.

10. **More impulsive**

Younger teens are generally more impulsive and spontaneous than their older peers. In class, we might notice that they sometimes do and say things that appear thoughtless or insensitive. Older teens, with greater life experience, are generally more tactful and measured, and usually have better social skills.

10 ways that teenagers are different from adult learners

We have already seen that teenage students respond well to being treated like adults. It is important to remember, though, that there are many ways in which teenagers are significantly different from grown-ups.

The following characteristics are not necessarily true of all older teenagers, but they should be taken into consideration by teachers who have decided to approach their teenage students in the same way they would approach a group of adult learners.

1. Less likely to empathise with the teacher

Teenage students are more likely to consider their teacher an authority figure, and do not see themselves as their teacher's social equals in the same way that adult students might. This can mean that they are more deferential or passive when it comes to negotiating learning, or that it is harder for them to empathise with the teacher's aims and perspectives than it is for adult learners.

2. Less willing to ask for help

Adult learners tend to be more confident about asking for help or indicating that they do not understand something in class. Teenagers, on the other hand, are more likely to stay silent and try to muddle through the best they can. Be aware of this, and take steps to ensure that teenagers have access to extra explanations and support when you sense that it might be appropriate.

3. More inclined to take risks

The teenage years are associated with risk-taking, and this can have both positive and negative consequences in the language classroom. The teenage attitude of 'let's-see-what-happens' can mean that lessons are enriched by students' spontaneous ideas and off-the-cuff remarks, but it can also result in slapdash work and a less methodical approach to studying.

4. Less autonomous

With greater life skills and learning experience, adult students are generally better equipped to find the resources they need to learn independently outside the classroom. Teenagers need more guidance. Remember to discuss study skills with your teenage students, and share techniques to help them become more autonomous in their learning (see Unit 21).

5. More willing to accept uncertainty

Teenagers are generally less concerned with the gaps in their knowledge and understanding than their adult counterparts. For example, you might find that teenagers have better gist reading skills, simply glossing over the unknown words they encounter in a reading text. Adult learners, on the other hand, often want to know the meaning of every new word straight away.

6. More likely to switch off in class

The motivation of teenage students is often less clear-cut than that of adult students. Whereas many adult students are instrumentally motivated to learn English for better life and career prospects, and have signed up – and paid – for their English classes with a determination to get the most out of them, the situation with teenagers is hazier. In many cases, teens take English classes because they have to, or because a family member is paying for them to do so. As a result, they are less likely to be self-driven, and more likely to drift when they are not in the mood to learn.

7. Less interested in grammar and language analysis

As exams approach, older teenage students begin to take an interest in grammar practice and language analysis activities, but generally speaking these are not things that they enjoy in their own right. For that reason, lessons with teenagers always need to have a strong communicative element. Adult learners on the other hand, tend to be interested in both analysing language and communicating in English.

8. Less skilled at managing their time

Teenagers often underestimate how much time they are going to need to complete a task, and also have a tendency to put things off. This can lead to late assignments and rushed work. Give them plenty of advance notice and reminders to help them get their work done on time. Adult learners, despite their busy schedules and out-of-class commitments, usually have much better time-management skills.

9. More emotional

Although mature in many ways, older teenagers find it harder to regulate their emotions than adults, and are sometimes hampered in their learning by their emotional states. Adults are usually – but not always – better at leaving the problems of everyday life at the classroom door.

10. Better mobile-phone etiquette

We often complain that teenagers are obsessed with their devices, but they are much better than adults at remembering to switch off their phones in class, and deserve credit for this. When a phone rings unexpectedly in the middle of the lesson, it is most likely to be the teacher's. If we are going to lay down the law about the use of mobile phones in class, we need to make sure that our own phone is switched off first.

10 things that teenagers value in their teachers

It can take time to gain the respect of a group of teenage students, no matter how good the teacher's intentions are. One of the reasons for this slow process is that teenagers tend to feel slightly threatened by new teachers, and so can be quite cautious and reactive when they encounter them for the first time. Teenagers are not usually keen to articulate the things that they value in a teacher, partly because – unlike adult learners – they are less confident in their status as 'equal partners' in the classroom and so tend not to make suggestions, instead preferring to wait and see how the teacher wishes to work.

On the other hand, teenagers are very quick to express dissatisfaction with working methods and tasks, even if they cannot always offer an explanation as to why they do not like them or suggest a better alternative. By noticing the things that teenage students resent in a teacher's working methods, it's sometimes possible to figure out what they actually value.

Unit 4

1. Willingness to experiment

Although teenagers certainly prefer a well-prepared and methodical teacher to one who is unprepared and disorganised, a little bit of novelty and creativity will also go down well. When teens complain that a lesson is 'boring', what they actually mean is that it is predictable. Try to find a new twist on revision activities rather than always doing them in the same way. (See, for example, Unit 34.3: Mini-interviews from workbook questions.)

2. Consistency

For all that they value novelty and innovation in language-learning activities, teenagers do want predictability and consistency from their teachers when it comes to managing the classroom and handling evaluation. Don't spring surprise tests on them, for example, or go back on your word about lesson content.

3. Fairness

Teenagers have the capacity to endure uninspiring lessons without getting frustrated or upset, but they will never forgive a teacher for a perceived act of unfairness. Pay special attention to how you treat students, making sure that no one receives preferential or discriminatory treatment. Avoid double standards: if student A gets into trouble for not doing the homework on Monday, but student B is let off with a smile the next day for the same oversight, the rest of the group will rightly be annoyed.

4. Willingness to use technology

Don't feel intimidated by teens' mastery of technology. They are actually more interested in our attitudes towards technology than our ability to master it ourselves. Naturally, teens respect those teachers who already use technology as well as they do, but they are also generally happy to explain and demonstrate apps and programs to less tech-aware teachers – provided we show a genuine interest and willingness to learn.

5. Not embarrassing students

Avoid comments that put individual students in embarrassing situations. Teenagers are highly concerned with how other people see them, and are particularly aware of the danger of losing face in front of their classmates. Insensitive comments by teachers (about a new hairstyle, clothes, pronunciation, test results, etc.) can make teenagers cringe – even if the comment itself is positive or seemingly innocuous. Remember that teenagers are not really interested in winning the approval of the teacher: it's the other students in the class whose opinions matter to them. Keep personal comments to a minimum. Teenage students notice if we respect them in this way, and tend to respect us back as a result.

6. Curiosity about their interests

When teenage students do talk about their interests in class, it can be demoralising if the teacher does not show much curiosity or interest. Such an attitude comes across as belittling and dismissive. If teenage students are particularly engaged by a topic that is of personal interest to them, encourage them – but do not require them – to bring in some extra information about the topic to the next lesson, or to do a mini-presentation on the topic. It is not necessary to share the student's enthusiasm, merely to show interest and to pay attention.

7. Sensitivity to students' schedules

Teenagers often have tough daily schedules, with a number of different teachers of other subjects all making demands of them at the same time. A common complaint among teens is that a teacher 'only thinks about his/her own subject'. Rather than announcing the date of a test, for example, ask the class in advance which day would suit them best, and try to come up with an arrangement that works for everyone. You might try the class-rep technique for this (see Unit 14.1).

8. Willingness to negotiate

As noted above, teenage students appreciate it when teachers demonstrate flexibility and a willingness to negotiate with them. In addition to giving plenty of advance notice when it comes to announcing tests and out-of-class assignments, bear in mind that teens respond well to being given options and being allowed to take responsibility for their own learning.

9. Setting an example

Teenagers expect their teachers to live up to the standards that they set for their students. For example, if it isn't acceptable for students to say that they didn't have time to do the homework, teenage students will resent it when we say that we didn't have time to correct the assignments that we promised to have ready for the lesson.

10. Ending the class on time

Resist the temptation to take another minute or two at the end of the lesson to finish an activity or explanation. Break times are precious for teenagers, and every second counts. Keep an eye on the clock and make sure you let the students go as soon as the bell goes at the end of class.

10 ways to find out about your teenage learners

Make an effort to find out about your teenage students. Try to discover what their learning needs and preferences are, why they are studying English, what they hope to achieve, but also something unrelated to school. The more relevant information we have about our students, the easier it is to plan lessons and learning activities that they will enjoy.

Teenagers really appreciate it when their teachers show an interest in them, and this can help to build a positive classroom dynamic. On the other hand, we should remember not to go too far. Teenagers are guarded about their private lives. We have no right to interrogate them or to demand that they share personal information.

The ideas below are all ways in which teachers can get to know their students better.

1. Set a personal example

Sharing information needs to be reciprocal. If we want our teenage students to provide us with information about themselves, we first need to set an example by telling the students relevant information about ourselves.

2. Ask questions

Keep questions simple and provide options for them to choose from. Don't be too direct. Questions such as *What kinds of learning activities do you prefer?* or *What do you want to do when you leave school?* are often too broad. Instead, narrow things down by providing options, for example:

Do you prefer [activity-type A] or [activity-type B]?

Rank these jobs in order of preference.

As you discuss their answers, other further useful information tends to emerge.

3. Listen to what they say

There is little point in asking questions if we don't listen to what students say. Really pay attention when students are talking about themselves. Look at them, listen carefully, and perhaps ask a follow-up question to demonstrate that you have been listening. Thank them for their answer.

4. Keep your eyes open

There are countless ways we can pick up snippets of information about students in the course of a lesson just by watching them. Notice what students are doing when they enter the classroom. Pay attention to the social interaction between members of the group. Watch students as they do pairwork or individual tasks (see Unit 15.9). Notice how well they listen to others. Take note of what they do when they have finished a task.

5. Ask them to share a website

Ask students to share a website that they think is useful or interesting. It can be a general website, or one connected to English learning. If you have the technology in your classroom, get each student to load the website they have chosen and say a few words about it. If you have an online class group set up, get students to post the link there.

6. Get them to write you a letter of introduction

This traditional technique is a good, if slightly old-fashioned way of getting information about your students. Tell students that you would like them to introduce themselves to you in a letter. Explain that the letter will help you to find out useful information about them, both as learners and as individuals. Ask them to tell you about themselves in their letter, focusing on information that is interesting (for example, favourite leisure activities) and useful (for example, number of years spent learning English, or plans for the future). Tell them not to include information that is obvious (for example, which school they attend) or irrelevant (for example, names and ages of their parents). Do the activity in class rather than setting it as a homework task in order to demonstrate that you value the information enough to dedicate lesson-time to gathering it. Keep the letters and re-read them throughout the year. The students normally put a lot of effort into them and they often contain some very useful information.

7. Create an online group

Set up a class group on an online educational platform or through social media. Use this as a way of communicating with students between lessons and as a way of sharing links and relevant information. You could ask students to post their opinions about a link you have added; alternatively, you could ask them a question in connection with using the internet for group communication (for example, to find out how many other online groups they belong to). This will give you an idea of how accustomed they are to online communication; it will also give you some information about their other interests and commitments.

8. Post a survey or poll

Use a survey generator (such as Google forms or Survey Monkey) to create a survey with relevant questions for the students to answer. Alternatively, use the polling function in your online group to find out students' opinions and preferences.

9. Get them to post a message

As an alternative to tip 6, get students to send you their introductory letter as a direct message in your online group.

10. Ask them to post a video

As a further alternative to writing about themselves, ask students to film themselves talking about their interests, hobbies, etc. They can send the finished video to you in the class group.

10 questions to ask teenagers

Ask teenage students the questions from this unit at the beginning of the year, or after you have had a few lessons together. If it is a new group, some of the questions will give students a chance to reflect on past learning experiences with different teachers. If you have already been working with the group for a year or more, the questions will provide a structure with which they can provide ongoing feedback.

Questions can be asked face-to-face in class, where they can provide the basis for small-group discussions. Alternatively, invite students to hand in written answers to the questions, or to post them to your online class group, if you have one.

In order to help students reflect on past lessons, try brainstorming the different activities they can remember doing. Students can work together to make posters, mind maps or lists, which can then be referred to when students answer the questions.

See page 140 of the Appendix for a photocopiable list of the questions.

Unit 6

1. What was your least favourite lesson last year? Why?

As you go through the responses, try to notice the main reasons cited: was it connected to topic choice, language level, working mode, or something else?

2. What was your favourite lesson last year? Why?

Again, see if you can draw conclusions from the answers given that can help you to identify a winning formula for planning lessons that work well.

3. What would you like us to stop doing in English lessons? Why?

Students usually select an activity type, often connected to assessment, but occasionally they pick up on our classroom-management habits as well.

4. What would you like us to keep doing in English lessons? Why?

This is a way of finding out which activities and techniques our students value.

5. What do you think it would be worth trying out in English lessons? Why?

This provides students with a window to make suggestions, perhaps based on good techniques that they have experienced with other teachers. Very often students just say 'Everything's OK the way it is', but it's always worth asking this question as they will be unlikely to say what they feel otherwise.

6. If you could choose, would you prefer to spend more time or less time learning English? Why?

This is a deceptively simple question, which can actually elicit all manner of opinions and reactions from students. Reading their answers will give us insights into the students' attitudes and motivation levels, and it may also tell us something about the effect that our own teaching is having.

7. Which is the hardest day of the week for you at school? Why?

This is useful information to know, especially if you have an English lesson with the group on that particular day. You might want to make sure that you don't set deadlines or schedule tests to fall too regularly on this day of the week.

8. What is your opinion of the homework you get?

The answers you get should give you an idea of the students' opinion about the quantity and quality of out-of-class tasks that they are given.

9. What do you wish the teacher knew about you?

You never know how students are going to respond to this question. The answers you get can be facetious or serious. It's a question worth asking, though: sometimes students have something they want to get off their chest, and this question enables them to do it.

10. Is there anything you want to ask the teacher?

As above, this question is deliberately framed to be as open as possible. Students might ask questions about your plans for the year, they might make requests, or they might ask a personal question.

"I ask students questions to help them become more aware of their own learning strategies. For example, asking students if they are better at remembering written words or spoken sounds can help them to start noticing their own strengths and weaknesses."

Diana Granado, Colombia

10 things to avoid when working with teenagers

It is not always easy to teach in such a way that teenagers respect and appreciate our efforts, but it is very easy to pick up habits that work against us. With teenagers, the key thing to remember is their strong sense of justice. It is particularly important not to make decisions in the classroom that appear to be unfair, or to make assumptions about students which they feel to be ungrounded. Many of the ideas in this unit are concerned with avoiding such situations.

As teachers, we also have a serious responsibility to ensure that the students are under proper supervision during lesson time. Teenagers enjoy taking risks and acting recklessly in front of their friends, so we need to make sure that students' safety is never in jeopardy during the lesson. Accordingly, this unit also looks at avoiding situations in which the teacher could be held to account for not supervising students properly.

1. Arriving late for class

Our responsibility for the students begins when the bell rings for the start of the lesson, so get there in plenty of time. This is particularly important if the students are already in the classroom when the lesson begins. If an incident occurs after the bell and we are not there, we are potentially at fault.

2. Being influenced by the opinions of others

Our colleagues can be full of advice when they find out that we are about to start teaching a certain group of teenagers. They might say *Watch out for [Student A] – she's/he's a handful!* or *They're really smart, so work them hard.* Although such advice is well intended, it can lead to us having pre-conceived ideas about students we have not even met. It is best to be sceptical about such advice and to concentrate on treating each new class on its own merits. In any case, it is quite common for teenage groups to behave quite differently with different teachers.

3. Labelling students

Teachers sometimes fall into the trap of labelling certain students, perhaps based on first impressions, or maybe even based on their clothes, hairstyle or physical appearance. Avoid this counter-productive tendency, and keep an open mind about teenagers. An especially negative consequence of so-called 'labelling theory' is that it can lead to self-fulfilling prophecies: the teacher decides that a student is lazy, the student senses this, resents it, and stops trying.

4. Judgements about talent or ability

Try to promote a healthy growth mindset in your teenage students. Don't tell students that they're *smart*, *intelligent*, or *great at English* – praise them instead for working hard or being curious about the language. Similarly, never tell teenagers that they are *untalented* or *weak* – talk instead about the need to find an approach that works for them. (See Unit 20 for ideas about working with mixed-ability classes.)

5. Physical distance between the students and you

Teenagers sometimes try to put as much distance as they can between the teacher and themselves. Closer proximity makes communication easier, improves the classroom dynamic, and reduces the likelihood of discipline problems. Don't let teenage students fill up the classroom from the back row forwards. If there are empty spaces at the front, get students in the back to move forward. (See Unit 9.4).

6. Leaving the class mid-lesson

Just as arriving late for class is inadvisable, so is leaving teenage students unattended during a lesson. Occasionally you might realise in the middle of a class that you have left something on your desk in the staffroom. Don't go back for it yourself; instead, ask a responsible student to go and get it for you.

7. Springing unpleasant surprises

Don't give students unannounced tests or decide, spontaneously, to award a grade for the homework teenagers have just handed in. Similarly, do not call up individual students to give an oral presentation unless they have been warned in advance.

8. Comparing them to other groups

Teenagers hate it when the teacher compares them unfavourably to other groups, so don't say things like *I don't see what the fuss is about: I did this with 10B last week and they had no problems.* It never has the intended motivating effect, and merely fosters a sense of resentment.

9. Asking for information you don't actually want

Do yourself a favour and don't ask a question if you don't want to know the answer. If two distracted teenagers are doing something under the desk, asking *What are you doing?* is not a smart move. You actually don't want to know. Far better to say *Can you stop that, please?*

10. Losing your temper

Whatever happens, keep your cool. When emotions become strained in the classroom, we need to remain calm and assertive. Losing your temper with a class usually only adds additional strain to the situation and makes resolving problems even harder.

> *"Coolness is in the eye of the beholder. So no matter how cool and eclectic you think your music collection is, your students won't agree with you. Let them find language forms in the music that they like and they'll be much more engaged."*
>
> **Donal Fogarty, University of San Gil. Colombia**

10 things to remember when planning lessons for teenage students

Two important elements of planning successful lessons are anticipation and flexibility. As you look through the materials for the forthcoming lesson, try to assess how appropriate you think the topic and tasks are for your teenage students, and make selected changes to the standard Teacher's Book lesson as necessary.

Once the lesson has begun, it is important to give yourself options. Given that teenagers' reactions to topics and activities often take us by surprise, it is worth getting into the habit of developing a flexible approach that leaves some room for manoeuvre. There is no reason to lock yourself into your own lesson plan. If something is going unexpectedly well, it makes sense to capitalise on that through extension and follow-up. If something is going badly, you might want to question the wisdom of soldiering on and consider alternative courses of action.

1. It's OK to overrule the Teacher's Book

The Teacher's Book might suggest an activity which, based on previous experience, you know the students are going to struggle with or dislike. A common example from the teenage classroom is reading texts out loud, which teenagers find difficult, time-consuming, embarrassing, and of questionable language-learning value. Try to re-work the activity to make it more student-friendly, rather than soldiering on with a task that is guaranteed to be unpopular.

2. Don't ask questions that are too personal

A common way of activating new language in controlled practice is providing students with personal questions to answer. As you read the questions in the lesson plan and think of further questions yourself, make sure that the questions you are going to ask are not too personal or prying. Teenagers can be very protective of their private lives.

3. Controversial topics need sensitive handling

In some teenage groups, a high level of language proficiency is offset by low levels of personal maturity. Be careful when dealing with potentially controversial topics, such as immigration or national stereotypes. Don't introduce such topics unless you know that the students will be able to deal with them in a measured, constructive and diplomatic way. Test the waters first, and, if necessary, put lessons that focus on controversial topics on hold until the students are mature enough to handle them.

4. Check that students' links and clips are appropriate

If students have been asked to give a presentation in which they show a video clip, check it first to make sure that its content is above board and appropriate for the language classroom. Teenagers are often poor judges of what belongs in the classroom and what does not.

5. Plan lessons in context

Bear in mind the time of day and the day of the week when planning lessons for teenagers, taking into consideration any factors that might affect how well the students are able to focus on the content of the lesson. For example, if the English lesson is right after a PE lesson, don't schedule a test for that day: students will be tired, flustered, and rushing to get to class on time.

6. Involve students in planning decisions

Broadcast your plans for upcoming lessons and give students the chance to express their opinions or make suggestions about content or scheduling. Teenagers appreciate this gesture from their teachers, and often have plenty of constructive things to say.

7. Be honest about difficulties

Planned lessons can go badly for a variety of reasons, and often we are not sure ourselves what has gone wrong. Make the effort to investigate. Talk about it with the students. *This isn't going very well, is it?* is not only an honest thing to say, it can also be very constructive. Teenagers respect this kind of honesty from the teacher, and in many cases will open up about the difficulties they are having with an activity. It is then sometimes possible to rescue the lesson by making changes to the lesson plan mid-class.

8. Seize unexpected openings

Sticking too rigidly to the lesson plan can cause us to miss opportunities for authentic communication with teenagers. Don't be afraid to pursue a topic with follow-up questions if students are responding with more enthusiasm than we expected. Similarly, if something unexpected happens during the lesson (for example, a bird lands on the classroom window sill), resist the temptation to restore order and instead explore the communicative potential of the situation, for example, by asking students to describe what they saw, heard or felt.

9. Give appropriate deadlines

The one aspect of our lesson planning that teenagers are sure to take a keen interest in is the scheduling of tests and assignments. Make sure that you give students adequate time to prepare for tests, and try to reach an agreement about the best day of the week to schedule them for. Teenagers are quick to complain if they feel that they are being unfairly burdened with work.

10. Learn from lesson-planning mistakes

An unsuccessful lesson is not the end of the world, and needn't be a reason to despair. Reflect on lessons that don't go as well as planned, perhaps by writing down a few thoughts at the end of the day. Think about what you would change to the lesson plan in the light of what happened, and consider how you will teach the lesson differently next time.

"I think of teaching as 'eventful' rather than 'stressful' – above all I plan to be surprised by my students!"

Hoang Thi Khanh Tam, Hue University, College of Foreign Languages, Vietnam

10 ways to use the space in the classroom

Unlike young learners, teenagers are used to sitting down in lessons, and have less need – and less desire – for activities which constantly get them on their feet and moving around. Having said that, teenagers do have a lot of pent-up energy, and it can be exhausting for them to spend long periods of time sitting at their desks. A good policy is to aim for at least one activity a lesson that breaks the monotony of static seating arrangements and provides a bit of variety.

Seating arrangements can help or hinder communication in the classroom. This unit offers different options to try out. Teenagers are also sensitive to how the teacher manages the physical dimensions of the classroom and, in particular, the distance between them and other students during activities. It is also worth noting that changing the distance between ourselves and a student can have an impact on how they respond to prompts and questions.

Many of the ideas below are designed for classrooms where the desks can be moved around. If this is not possible in your classroom, look for ways to modify some of the activities so that they can be used in the space at the front of the room.

1. Get students to sit somewhere different

Teenagers enjoy the security of sitting in the same seat next to the same classmates in every lesson, but it is occasionally worth asking them to change places for the duration of one pairwork activity. The novelty of working with a different partner can energise the interaction between students, while the physical effort required to stand up and move to a different part of the room is sometimes enough to break teenagers' lethargy. After the activity, let students go back to where they were sitting before, which also provides a bit more movement.

2. Use a horseshoe seating arrangement

In classes with 15 students or fewer, arrange the desks in the shape of a horseshoe, or letter C. This enables students to see one another's faces as well as the board. It also improves the quality of spoken interaction among students, mainly because it is easier to follow what the speaker is saying when you can see their face.

3. Create islands

For larger groups, arrange pairs of desks into islands, each one seating four or five students. Islands are ideal for groupwork and pairwork, and also make it easy for the teacher to get around the room. Be aware that putting students directly opposite each other in this way has its disadvantages, too. Teenagers sitting at islands tend to chat to each other and engage in off-task behaviour more readily than if they are seated in a horseshoe arrangement or in rows.

4. Offer front-row privileges

If the classroom is organised into rows of desks, teenagers often head straight for the back of the room, leaving an empty row at the front. To counteract this, offer special privileges to the people who volunteer to sit in the front row, such as not having to answer a question, or being able to leave the classroom first at the end of the lesson.

5. **Form a circle**

The technique of 'circle time' is mainly associated with young learners, but it can also be modified effectively for use with teenagers. Arrange all the chairs in a circle in the middle of the room, with the teacher and students all taking their place in the circle. Use this technique at the beginning of lessons in which the students will be working independently of the teacher for the whole class. Use it again at the end to share findings and reflect on learning outcomes. This technique is particularly effective with more mature or older teenage students.

6. **Spread out, speak up**

This fun, energising technique is designed to help timid teenagers speak louder and more assertively. Before beginning a paired speaking task, ask each pair to stand up and move apart from each other until there is a distance of at least five metres between them. As the task begins, play some music. Students really have to raise their voices in order to be heard. Naturally, this activity generates a lot of noise, which is precisely the aim.

7. **Let students stand up**

A simple change of posture can bring relief to jaded teenagers, even if there is not enough space in the classroom for them to move around. Before beginning a pairwork activity, ask students to stand up and do the task on their feet.

8. **Try a fishbowl discussion**

Place four chairs in the centre of the room. Place all the other chairs around them in an outer circle. Invite four students to do a speaking task or have a discussion in the middle. Give the students in the outer circle specific listening tasks. (See page 141 of the Appendix for sample listener roles for use in fishbowl discussions.)

9. **Don't sit behind your desk**

Sitting behind the teacher's desk creates a physical barrier between you and the students. It makes it harder for you to notice what is happening in the classroom and also signals to the students that you are unavailable. The moment you stand up, teenagers become more attentive. They are also much more likely to ask for help from a teacher who is standing up than from one who is sitting down, as they know you can approach them more easily.

10. **Don't tower over students**

Teenagers can be intimidated by teachers standing over them as they work. Asking *Any questions?* Or *How are you getting on here?* is fine, but if you're really interested in engaging with students in these situations, make yourself smaller. Find a chair next to the students or crouch down slightly. Teenagers find it easier to talk to us when we're down at their level.

In the classroom

The following section looks at the teacher's role as a manager and facilitator of classroom interaction. One of the things that it is important to acknowledge when working with teenage students is the fact that in many cases the students do not arrive in class with high levels of motivation to take part. The teacher's handling of the lesson can therefore be crucial. This section looks at the importance of establishing motivation at the start of each lesson, and considers the ways in which effective classroom management – establishing clear goals, engaging students' curiosity with questions and implementing a variety of interactive working modes – can give students both the desire to 'switch on' and the confidence to take part.

Many of the tips and activities in this section are based on exploiting the benefits of collaborative and interactive working modes. Although pairwork and groupwork activities can be extremely engaging for teenage students, we need to be aware that there is much that can go wrong when teens are working together. It is therefore important to make sure that we have first established positive norms for interpersonal communication, and this inevitably involves community-building work in the classroom. For this reason, this section also focuses on ways that we can build rapport with teenage students. Although there are no guarantees that we will be able to establish a harmonious classroom environment with every teenage group we teach, it is possible to identify positive steps that a teacher can take to promote mutual understanding and to reduce the chances of resentment building up between the students and the teacher, and between individual members of the class.

When things do go wrong in the classroom (as from time to time they inevitably do) it is easy to become frustrated. We often forget that the decisions we take in the classroom will ripple into subsequent lessons and have an impact on shaping the future learning environment of the classroom. This unit therefore takes a positive and proactive stance on dealing with behaviour problems.

We are all familiar with the methodological dilemmas presented by mixed-ability classrooms and the challenges of getting teenage students to think critically and to develop effective study skills. The units that follow adopt a positive approach to teaching teenagers, which involves regarding gaps in knowledge and mismatches between students as opportunities to embrace rather than hurdles to overcome.

10 ways to begin lessons with teenagers

The start of the lesson is a vital phase of the class, as it sets the tone for what is to follow. Teenagers' lives are often stressful and complicated, so they can be preoccupied when they arrive for the start of the lesson – something teachers sometimes misread: to us they can simply seem distracted or demotivated. The teacher's job is to bring everyone together and establish a positive focus for the class. Beginning the lesson in a meaningful and memorable way can harness attention, instil motivation and pave the way for effective learning. The following simple techniques can all be used with a group of teenagers to start the lesson in a positive way.

1. Welcome them to the class

Start on a positive note. If possible, stand near the classroom door and greet students as they enter. Welcome each student with a smile, looking to make eye contact. If students are already in the room when you arrive in class, greet them verbally (e.g. *Welcome to the class, everyone!*), getting their attention in an assertive and non-confrontational way. Commands (e.g. *Listen up!*) are best avoided.

2. Give them time to settle

Teenagers need time to settle at the start of the lesson. Give them a few moments to finish whatever they were doing prior to the lesson, without becoming impatient. A time warning (e.g. *You've got another 30 seconds*) can be a very effective way of helping teenagers manage this transition from break time to lesson time.

3. Check in with students

Get into the habit of reaching out to students with a few questions or comments before the lesson begins. Showing that you are available (e.g. *Does anyone have anything they want to ask?*) and demonstrating that you have been paying attention to their lives (e.g. *How was yesterday's History test?*) can help establish empathy and co-operation with teenagers.

4. Tell a quick story or anecdote

Teenagers are more interested in the teacher's life than we sometimes imagine. Share a relevant short anecdote or story at the start of the lesson about something that happened to you recently (e.g. *You know the new supermarket in town? I was standing in line there yesterday, when …*) This can be a great way to get students' attention and can also generate authentic English-language interaction with the class.

5. Assign special roles

Use the time at the start of the lesson to assign certain students special roles and responsibilities for the lesson, for example, setting up the projector, keeping time, or handing out extra materials. You can either encourage students to volunteer for these roles (e.g. *Is there anyone who has a watch? I need someone to be the timekeeper…*), or nominate individual students in recognition of their strengths and interests (e.g. *[Student A], you're good with technology; could you help me with the projector today?*) For more on student roles, see Unit 14.

6. Spark their curiosity

Give students something to notice as they walk into the classroom. This can be a puzzle or riddle written on the board, a small change to the classroom seating arrangements, or even an unusual object on the teacher's desk. Teenagers are curious by nature, and will often ask *What's that on the board?* or *Why is there a pineapple on your desk?* Elicit their ideas and encourage them to guess. This can be an effective lead-in to the topic of that day's lesson.

7. Set specific goals

Use the beginning of the class to remind students of their goals for that day's class. Be specific. The goal might be a particular outcome (e.g. getting an answer to a key question), a process (e.g. working in pairs harmoniously), or even an attitude towards learning (e.g. keeping their phones in their bags). If the goal is achieved, reward students with the activity of their choice (see tip 10). If there were behaviour problems in the previous class, use the start of the lesson to establish and articulate the norms and expectations for the class ahead, focusing on positives rather than negatives (see Unit 19.3).

8. Signpost the learning ahead

Use the board to write up key goals or areas to focus on at the start of the lesson, and refer back to it as the lesson unfolds, and again at the end of the lesson. One technique is to write a question on the board at the start of the class that the students should be able to answer by the end of the lesson.

9. Ask a bonus-point question

Give students the chance to win a bonus point at the start of the lesson by correctly answering a quiz question that you ask them. The question can refer back to the content of the previous lesson, or can be a general knowledge or current affairs question. Keep track of how many bonus points each student has from lesson to lesson, and reward them with a classroom privilege or a good grade once they have collected five bonus points.

10. Give them something to look forward to

Teenagers often have off-topic requests at the start of the lesson, e.g. *Can we play a game? / Can we listen to music? / Can I show everyone this video I found on YouTube?* Negotiate these requests at the start of the lesson, promising to find time for one activity later in the lesson if – and only if – they successfully meet their goals for that day's class (see tip 7). This is an excellent way to keep students focused and on-task throughout the class.

10 ways to ask questions effectively

Teenage students can initially be reluctant to answer questions in class, especially if they sense that there is a chance that they might lose face. Answers can be short and cautious as a result. Try to give your questions the dynamic of an invitation to speak rather than a request to demonstrate knowledge; allow teenage students to see that your questions are not designed to try to trap or trick them. A good principle to follow is to avoid display questions – questions that the teacher already knows the answer to – and instead to use open-ended questions that allow students to express a variety of information or opinions.

Some of the following questioning techniques are designed to avoid putting students under pressure; others look at ways we can motivate students to answer by providing them with space or by giving them options.

1. Use open questions

Use open questions to draw students in. Open questions are subjective and have more than one possible answer, depending on the opinion of the speaker; closed questions, on the other hand, are more concerned with what is objectively true and therefore usually have only one correct answer. So instead of asking *Who built the castle we read about in the text?* try *What was the most interesting thing you learned from this text?*

2. Signpost your questions

The teacher usually spends a lot of time talking in lessons, and teenagers rarely pay unbroken attention. As a result, they often miss the moment that questions are asked in class, and are then surprised to find the teacher looking at them expectantly. Signpost important questions in class. Say *So here's my question...* or *This brings us to a big question....*

3. Make use of waiting time

Resist the temptation to answer your own questions. If no one volunteers, wait a few seconds, scanning the room. Instead of looking right at the students' faces, focus on the space just above their heads. This is significantly less intimidating for teenagers than being stared at by the teacher. After four or five seconds, rephrase the question if necessary.

4. Write the question on the board

Writing the question up on the board where everyone can see it is another way of making use of waiting time. It also indicates to students that the question is not going to go away.

5. Phrase questions as invitations

When nominating students to answer a question, use indirect techniques. Teenagers respond well to a slightly playful, invitational approach. Instead of *[Student A], what's your answer?* try saying *[Student A], you look like you have an interesting answer to this question ...* or *[Student A], do you have anything you want to add?* Asking questions in this way not only encourages students to speak, it also provides them with a face-saving way of declining the invitation.

6. Use random techniques to nominate

Write each student's name on a lollipop stick and put all the sticks in a jar. Occasionally, instead of nominating a student yourself, choose a name at random from the jar. This keeps students on their toes, and develops teenagers' ability to respond to a question when they are not sure of the answer. Use this technique sparingly at first, and discuss it with your teenage students. If they can see its benefits, use it more regularly.

7. Give students options

When a student has been nominated to answer a question (as above), include the option of not having to answer the question (or answering it later). Asking *Do you want to speak, pass, or nominate?* is one way of doing this. If students do not want to speak, they can pass, in which case you turn to another student. Alternatively, they can nominate someone else to answer. To many teachers' surprise, this technique works extremely well, and students choose to pass or nominate much less frequently than we might imagine. Students who have chosen to pass often put their hands up a few moments later, once they have had a chance to hear someone else's answer or to think about the question a bit longer themselves.

8. Ask students to answer on a scale of 1 to 5

When faced with a closed question, many teenagers simply say *I don't know* and sit back. To counteract this tendency, ask students to give an answer on a scale of 1 to 5, where 1 = *I have no idea, but I'll say ...*, 2 = *I don't really know, but it might be ...*, 3 = *I'm not sure. Maybe it's ...?*, 4 = *I'm pretty sure the answer is ...* and 5 = *I'm sure that the answer is ...* This technique encourages students to respond to prompts, and also helps them to acquire useful chunks of language. Most importantly, it encourages them to speculate.

9. Move forwards, then back

Be aware that your movement towards and away from a student can influence how well and how long that they speak for. Stepping towards a student after you ask a question is an effective way to get them speaking. Once the student begins speaking, taking a step back has the effect of indicating that you would like them to continue for a longer time, whereas standing still shows that you are satisfied with a short answer.

10. Phrase questions negatively for a better response

Many teenagers hate talking about what they love, but love talking about what they hate. Remember this when asking open questions. Instead of asking *Who's your favourite singer?* try *What's the worst song on YouTube?*

10 tips for motivating teenagers

Many teenage students – given the choice – would rather be somewhere else. As the lesson begins, teenagers have often not yet made up their minds whether or not to commit themselves: there is an aspect of wait-and-see. The start of the lesson, therefore, is when we need to establish a compelling reason for them to take part; otherwise there is a chance that they will zone out or begin doing something else under the desk.

With teenagers, it helps to think of motivation in terms of here-and-now. It's true that some teenage students – especially older ones – are driven by longer-term personal goals, such as passing exams. In most cases, however, the most effective way to motivate teenage students is to provide them with language-learning tasks that are intrinsically motivating, or worth doing in their own right.

1. Have a positive attitude

Set an example for your students with the way you approach the lesson. As you anticipate each class, find something in it that you can look forward to yourself – a reason to enjoy it. Teenagers can tell if their teacher is not making much of an effort, or is just going through the motions. If we ourselves are not enthused about the English lesson, why should they be?

2. Be organised

Make sure you are clear in your own mind about your plans for the lesson, and that you have all the materials you need set up on your desk, where students can see them. Be ready to 'sell' the lesson. Teenagers tend to make snap judgements at the start of class about what the teacher has planned. As they enter the room, they often ask, *What are we going to do today?* This is more than just mere curiosity: in many cases they are actively deciding whether or not it is worth paying much attention to our class that day.

3. Communicate clearly

Don't just drift into the activities of the lesson. Establish the goals for that day's class, and provide a clear rationale. Make sure the students know what they are going to do – and why it's worth doing. Communicate outcomes rather than procedures, and focus on meaning rather than form. For example, instead of saying *We're going to practise using the future perfect*, say *You're going to decide how life will have changed 50 years from now.* Write key challenges or outcomes on the board.

4. Create a relaxed, focused environment

The ideal state of mind for learning is one of relaxed alertness. Establishing the goals and outcomes for the lesson is one thing, but teenage students are only really able to focus on their learning if they are free from anxiety. For teenagers, anxiety in the classroom is often caused by not understanding what they have to do, or by the fear that the teacher has laid traps for them, such as making them do a surprise test, or forcing them to speak in front of the whole class. Before you begin the activities of the day, take the time to deal with students' questions, and reassure them that there are no nasty surprises in store for them.

5. **Spark students' curiosity**
Identify something interesting in that day's lesson content. Present it to students in the form of a puzzle. For example, if the class is going to read a text about an unaccompanied child on a plane, before they read the text, say to students: *A nine-year-old child got on a plane without a ticket or boarding pass and didn't get caught. How?* Discuss their ideas and suggestions. This not only motivates teenagers to read the text in question, it is also an effective way of eliciting key vocabulary.

6. **Set a challenge**
Give bored teenage students challenges as a way to motivate them in lessons. For example, when setting writing tasks, instead of giving a word limit of 'about 80 words', ask them to write 79 words exactly. Alternatively, if you are confident that you can always tell when your teenage students are using their mobile phones in class, set them the challenge of sending you an English-language text message during the lesson without your noticing. (This idea comes courtesy of Tibor Prievara.)

7. **Personalise language analysis**
Teachers generally have a more abstract interest in the English language and how it works than their teenage students. Instead of analysing language generically, personalise it as much as you can. One way of doing this is to use your students' names when presenting model grammar sentences to the class. This makes the language more real, and also raises a smile. Make sure that the sentences you use do not embarrass or patronise students.

8. **Establish routines**
When you find activities that your teenage students like, look for ways to ration their use in order to increase motivation. Build these popular, short activities into the routine of your teaching, so that there is always something for teenagers to look forward to in every lesson. Keep updating and refreshing your bank of classroom routines, being careful not to overuse the activities.

9. **Welcome students' questions**
Teenage students can be nervous about admitting that they do not understand something in class, and as a result are often reluctant to put their hands up to ask questions, leading to demotivation. Pause regularly to see if students have any questions, and thank them emphatically when they do. Make a point of saying *Thanks for the question* or *That's a great question*. This, in turn, gives other students the confidence to speak up.

10. **Be mindful of maintaining your own motivation**
Take steps to sustain your own motivation and freshness. Keep a teacher's journal, attend professional development seminars, join a local teacher's association or develop an online personal learning network (PLN).

10 ways to get teens using their first language in lessons

If you share the same first language (L1) as your teenage students, think hard before enforcing an 'English only' rule in the classroom. It's true that lessons with teens can be a headache when there is too much off-task talking in L1, and it's therefore understandable that some teachers discourage its use altogether.

The learners' first language can be a valuable resource, however. Rather than seeking to ban it, we should be looking for ways to regulate its use in such a way that it promotes language awareness and motivates students to communicate in English. Remember that it is entirely natural for teenagers to want to use L1 at times, and they can become frustrated if they are prevented from doing so by the teacher.

Being able to draw on the L1 also has its uses in groups where the students are from a variety of backgrounds and have different mother tongues. This is particularly true when students are reconstructing texts together from notes made individually in L1 (see Unit 13.5). The idea is not to use L1 instead of English, but to use the notes in L1 as a way of motivating students to speak English together more effectively. The students' notes might be in different languages, but they still need to communicate together in English in order to agree on how best to recreate the text's original English sense.

1. Use a reversible flag

Regulate students' use of their mother language by placing a two-sided flag on the board or on the classroom wall. Explain that one side of the flag represents the English language, and its flip side represents the students' first language. At specific points in the lesson, flip the flag over to the L1 side. This is the moment to give explanations, do housekeeping tasks, or to introduce an activity that involves some use of L1. As soon as this phase of the lesson is over, turn the flag back to the side that represents English.

2. Get students to repeat instructions in L1

When setting up a task, give the instructions in English first. Then ask a student to repeat the instructions in the L1. Confirm or correct the translation. Finally, reiterate the instructions in English.

3. Do bilingual dialogues with a mediator

Make roleplays and dialogues more accessible for all learners by designating language-specific roles. For example, in a roleplay involving a tourist and a shopkeeper, the tourist (Student A) speaks English only, the shopkeeper (Student B) speaks L1 only, and the mediator – a helpful passer-by (Student C) helps them to bridge the communication gap by acting as interpreter, speaking both languages in the process.

4. Practise roleplays in L1

Allow teenagers to try out roleplays and other speaking tasks in the L1 first, before trying them in English. Very often, they are stuck for ideas, or are not comfortable with the interpersonal or pragmatic requirements of the exchange. Practising in L1 first can provide teenagers with ideas, improve confidence, and help to identify language gaps.

5. Do a double translation

Get students to translate a passage from the coursebook into their L1. Collect their translations and keep them for a week or so. Return the texts to the students and ask them to translate them back into English. When they have finished their second translation, allow them to check their work against the original. Teenagers, who rarely show much interest in passages from coursebooks, will be unusually keen to see the original text and find out how well they did. The activity works equally well if the students do not all share a common L1.

6. Compare different translations

Get students to write a paragraph about themselves in the L1. When they have finished, ask them to exchange papers with a partner and to translate the text into English. Get them to check each other's work and make suggestions for improvements. Finally, as a basis for further comparison, ask them to put their original texts into an online translator program (such as Google Translate) and to compare the two English translations. Ask students to identify sections of the text that the translator tool has translated well, as well as problematic areas. Get students to note any other interesting discoveries, as well.

7. Switch languages on a DVD clip

Invite teenagers to bring in an English-language film to class on DVD, making sure that it also has a dubbed version in the L1. Play students a very short extract from the movie in English, and ask students to translate the interaction into L1 in pairs. Compare the different ideas and decide which one sounds best. Then play the same clip again in the L1 version, comparing the translation used in the dub with those produced by the students.

8. Explain a clip

In groups where students have a variety of L1 backgrounds, find a short audio clip or video clip in a language that also happens to be the L1 of a minority of the students (eg two or three students) in the group. Make sure that you understand the clip yourself, or that you have a reliable English translation of it. Play the clip to the whole group and ask them to say what they think is happening. Get the students who speak the language used in the clip to respond to all the guesses, and then to give further explanations as required.

9. Do a corridor interview

Invite five teenage students to use their mobile phones to record a short interview in their first language with someone at school. It could be a student from another class, a teacher, or another school employee. The interviewee should be someone that most or all of the members of the class know. Afterwards, get the student interviewers to translate their questions, as well as the answers they received, into English. In class, collect the names of all the interviewees and write them on the board. Ask each of the five interviewers in turn to read out the English translations of their interviews. Each time, invite the other members of the class to guess who was being interviewed. To check, play the original L1 interviews. Once the interviewees have been correctly identified, review the English translations of the interviews and correct the language as necessary.

10. Provide feedback on lessons and activities

If you speak the students' L1, invite them to use their L1 to provide feedback on activities used in the lesson. Being able to use their first language for this task frees teenage students up to communicate their ideas quickly, easily and with greater directness.

10 ways to give teenagers responsible roles

Think beyond language practice when it comes to assigning roles for your teenage students. Although many language-learning activities assign students roles which help to improve their English, there are also plenty of ways that teenagers can get a stronger sense of usefulness through performing responsible roles in the classroom that are not directly connected to the language-learning activities of the lesson.

Teenage students have a growing sense of maturity and respond well to being given responsibility. Giving students a greater sense of agency regarding classroom decisions can help to counteract passive attitudes and can also boost students' self-esteem.

The roles we give teenagers can be connected to helping the teacher to manage the classroom. We can also assign roles that include a certain amount of responsibility for presenting language-learning materials or providing key input for classroom activities. Finally, there is scope for roles that draw on students' knowledge of topic areas, or that channel the opinions they might have about how lessons are delivered.

1. Appoint a class rep

When negotiating with a group of teenage students, give one student the responsibility of being a spokesperson for the entire group. First, allow members of the group to air their views among themselves. Do not take part in this conversation or listen in. Then ask the spokesperson to represent the views of the entire class. Rotate the responsibility of being class rep from lesson to lesson.

2. Ask them to handle the tech

Teenage students are sometimes more skilled at handling the technology of the classroom than their teacher. A minority of teenagers are content to poke fun at teachers as we struggle with technology in lessons; most teenagers, however, are happy to share their expertise. Offer students who are keen to help the responsibility of being in charge of setting up equipment and cueing up digital content. Allow them to control the laptop or IWB, and extend additional out-of-class tech responsibilities to them as well, such as downloading or formatting materials that you plan to use in class.

3. Make use of special skills

Find out about your students' skills and interests, and seize opportunities in your lessons that allow them to showcase their talents. Teenage students with an interest in art, music or acting can be a huge asset in setting up and enriching language-learning activities, and they appreciate it when their abilities are put to meaningful use. These students are also much more likely to pay attention to the language content of an activity if they have had the chance to contribute to the task in a creative way.

4. Appoint a timekeeper

Negotiate time limits for activities with students. Ask: *How much time do you want to complete this task?* When you have agreed on a timescale, invite one of the students to be responsible for keeping time and informing the other others in the class how much time is left.

5. **Use students as activity fact-checkers**

Give students opportunities to be the highest authority on a subject. A simple way to do this is to ask a student to prepare a short talk or presentation about themselves. Ask the other students to listen and write down three facts about the speaker, based on what they heard. Get the students to read out their sentences to the speaker, who confirms or corrects the information they offer. Students reading out sentences are not allowed to repeat anything that someone else has already read out. Next, ask the class to make further guesses about the speaker. For example, if the speaker has said that she supports FC Barcelona, the class might guess that her favourite player is Lionel Messi. The speaker listens to all the predictions and then has the chance to say whether or not they were correct.

6. **Micro-teaching**

Offer students the opportunity to be the teacher for a small section of the lesson. Invite them to prepare a micro-teaching segment on an aspect of language and deliver it to the rest of the class. You might ask them to pre-teach selected vocabulary, or – for a slightly greater challenge – to explain a grammar point. Teenagers enjoy being given this kind of responsibility. A further benefit is that in preparing their micro-teaching, they familiarise themselves thoroughly with the language they have been given the task of presenting.

7. **Give students summarising and adjudicating duties**

Let students summarise discussions and decide the outcomes of debates. When setting up a discussion activity, ask two or more students to volunteer to take the role of summarisers. Their task is to listen to the ideas expressed by the speakers and summarise the main points made. In team debates, instead of judging the outcome yourself, delegate the responsibility to a small group of students.

8. **Give students research tasks**

Coursebook topics occasionally coincide with the special interests of particular students in the group. When this happens, invite the students concerned to gather additional material about the topic in the run-up to the lesson; they can then share this information with the rest of the group in class.

9. **Share online administration tasks**

If you have an online group for your teenage class on a platform such as Edmodo or on a social media site such as WhatsApp or Facebook, offer students the opportunity to share group-admin responsibilities with you. Encourage the students to be proactive when it comes to posting, sharing ideas and uploading useful learning resources for the rest of the group. For example, if you are covering the topic of advertising in class, ask students to upload a photograph of an advert they have seen that they think is effective, and give them the task of commenting on all the photos that have been uploaded.

10. Get students to carry out observation tasks

Occasionally, invite one or two student volunteers to observe the class from the back of the room. This can be particularly worthwhile if you are trying out something new in class and are curious about how well it is working. Teenage students are entitled to express their opinions about our lessons, and as members of the group they command a unique perspective as observers. Teenage students respond well to being entrusted with this kind of mature responsibility, and usually make very insightful observations. Make sure there is a clear focus for the observation to ensure that the data collected is useful. For example, you might be trying out the lollipop stick technique for nominating students (see Unit 11.6) The observation task can be structured, in which case observers are provided with a form to complete (see page 142 of the Appendix for an example); alternatively, the observation can be unstructured, in which case student observers are given a blank piece of paper and are free to note any comments they have in connection with the focus of the observation.

"I usually give the most disruptive students the role of my assistant; this way they always have something to do when they get bored and it gives me an opportunity to praise them a lot for their good work."

Sandra Vida, teacher, Slovenia

10 reasons to get teenagers working in small groups and pairs

Groupwork and pairwork activities enable students to work at their own pace and with greater freedom. They also provide an important break from the monotony of sitting and listening to the teacher, and from the dullness of working alone.

Plan groupwork and pairwork activities carefully. Anticipate problems. Make sure there is always a clear rationale and focus for the activity, and ensure that students understand their task. Don't get teenagers working in small groups and pairs for too long, or for no apparent reason: that's when the problems – loud talking in L1, off-task behaviour, etc. – usually arise.

This unit outlines why it makes sense to give teenage students the regular opportunity to work in small groups and pairs.

1. They get time to confer

Teenagers seem to have a much greater need than adults to confer with their friends about what is happening in the lesson. They will do this in class anyway, even if we ask them not to. Allow teenagers to confer together in a constructive and natural way by giving them tasks to carry out in pairs. Being able to work with a partner provides teens with a feeling of security and reassurance.

2. They can recharge their batteries

Use pairwork and groupwork activities when teenage students appear lethargic or passive. Having the chance to turn to a partner and complete a simple task often has the effect of re-energising tired students, provided they have both a clear sense of what they are supposed to do, and the confidence that they can get it done.

3. It provides variety

Try fluid pairwork activities, which involve getting students to work with a variety of different partners in a short period of time. One example of this is speed-dating (see Unit 25.8). This provides a useful basis for repetition of language in controlled-practice situations, with the added advantage of variety, which makes the task more interesting for teenage learners.

4. It reduces dependence on the teacher

Pairwork and groupwork activities can provide students with the chance to analyse language and discover rules for themselves. Before providing an explanation of a language point, give students a guided-discovery task in pairs or small groups. This can help them to become more autonomous and independent in their learning.

5. It takes the pressure off

Use pairwork formats to practise speaking and pronunciation. This allows students to practise the language without the anxiety associated with having to perform dialogues or to attempt the pronunciation of difficult sounds in front of an audience.

6. It enables peer-learning and peer-teaching

Teenagers are sometimes more receptive to guidance given to them by their classmates than to that which they receive from the teacher. Working in pairs and small groups enables students to support each other in their learning, and can lead to situations where students can consolidate their understanding of the language through interaction with their peers.

7. It engages different skills and strengths

Try to find tasks and activities that require both knowledge of the language and non-linguistic skills. For example, give students a quick glimpse of a picture containing many different objects, and ask them to remember as many of them as they can. As they work together in pairs or small groups, students will need to combine their knowledge of English vocabulary with their ability to recall the objects. Different students will have different areas of strength, but together they can complete the task.

8. It promotes social skills

Encourage students to work with different people each time they do a pairwork or groupwork activity. Although teenagers are inclined to form pairs and small groups with their friends and near-neighbours, working with new people provides an ideal opportunity to develop important social skills, and it helps teenagers to become more accepting of classmates who are not in their immediate circle of friends.

9. It gives the teacher a chance to observe

A key advantage of pairwork and groupwork activities is that the students are less aware of the teacher's presence in the room. This provides us with an opportunity to observe the students in an unobtrusive way. Watch the students from a distance, observing how individual teens behave when they think the teacher is not paying attention to them, and noticing how well pairs and groups of students work together. Such informal observations can be very revealing, and can help us to find out more about our teenage students.

10. It allows the teacher to provide feedback discreetly

Move around the room as students carry out pairwork and groupwork activities. Use this time to provide individual feedback and support to students as they carry out their task. Teenagers prefer getting remedial guidance and language support when they are not being watched by the rest of the class.

10 ways to get teenagers into small groups and pairs

Teenagers tend to approach activities based on getting them into small groups and pairs with an element of caution. They are less inclined than young learners to enjoy overly playful ways of being paired off, so avoid anything that might strike them as being too childish. They are also inclined to want to work with the same people all the time. While acknowledging their need for security, from time to time it makes sense to encourage them to leave their comfort zones. Try a sorting activity on these occasions, a number of which are included below.

Remember that sorting students randomly often results in pairs and small groups that contain a mixture of levels, strengths and personalities. Treat this as an opportunity to foster a sense of teamwork and co-operation among your teenage students, rather than trying to keep seemingly incompatible students apart.

1. Ask them to work with the people around them

Use this as your standard technique. It's simple and straightforward, and it's also the one that teenage students object to least. If we generally let students work with the people sitting next to them – who are also often their friends – it helps to establish goodwill between us and the students. This can act in our favour when we occasionally ask them to try something a bit different.

2. Draw names from a hat

Get each student to write their name on a slip of paper and form pairs or groups by drawing names at random from a hat. This entire task can be delegated to the students if you prefer. Alternatively, if you already have a jar of lollipop sticks with the students' names written on them (see Unit 11.6), draw the names at random from that to form the groups or pairs.

3. Get them to 'number off'

Get students into random groups quickly by asking them to 'number off'. First do the maths. If there are 18 students in the group and you want them to work in threes, you will need six groups. Going round the room sequentially, each student calls out their number, starting with 'one', going up to 'six', and then starting again at 'one'. Do this until all the students have been allocated a number. Then form groups by asking all the students with the same number to sit together.

4. Use coloured slips of paper

Use different coloured slips of paper to get students into groups. Hand out the slips to students randomly, or, if you prefer, select which students get which colour. Once they have received their colour, students work together with their classmates who have received slips of the same colour.

5. Use birthdays or name days

Ask students to get together with other students in the room who were born in the same month as them, or whose name day falls in the same month as theirs. This technique will not necessarily produce groups of uniform size, but students from larger groups can then volunteer to even out the numbers by switching groups. This technique also ensures a certain amount of mingling between students in the sorting phase.

6. Do find-your-partner activities

Prepare sets of paired cards (e.g. 'question + answer' or 'word + definition') and distribute them among the students, giving one card to each. For example, one card might contain the question *Where is PewDiePie from?* The answer, which is *Sweden*, will be on one of the other cards. Alternatively, you could put a vocabulary item on one card, e.g. *vlog*, and put its definition – *a website or social media account where a person regularly posts short videos* – on another card. Students have to find their partner by mingling among the group and sharing the information on their card. When pairs have identified each other, they sit down together to do whatever pairwork task follows. See page 144 of the Appendix for further examples of paired cards.

7. Try jigsaw grouping

Split the class into four groups (A, B, C and D), allowing students to form the groups themselves. Give each group a different short text to read and discuss. These short texts could be parts taken from a long text that has been divided into four, or four short texts on the same topic. When students in each group have had time to discuss their text, form mixed groups of four students, containing one student from each of the four original groups. Do this in stages, getting one student from each group to stand up so that they can easily see who their new partners are. Once this new group has found a place to sit down together, repeat the process, getting another student from each group to stand up, and so on. Once they are all arranged in their new groups, students discuss and compare the information contained in the four different texts.

8. Try pyramid grouping

Set up a discussion task in pairs. After a few minutes, ask the pairs to merge and form groups of four. Give them some more time to share views and continue the discussion. Then merge groups again, this time forming groups of eight students.

9. Try a gallery activity

Place six pictures on the walls around the classroom. Invite students to walk around looking at the pictures and to stand in front of their favourite one. Use this as the basis for forming groups, and continue with a groupwork activity based on the pictures.

10. Match students from opposing teams

After a two-team debate or game, ask students to pair off with a member from the opposing team.

10 ways to establish rapport with teenagers

Teenagers pay close attention not only to how we deal with them as individuals, but also to how we treat others in the group. In the crucial first few encounters with a teenage group, students will therefore be watching us carefully in order to gauge our attitudes.

The teacher has a central role in facilitating the development of a good rapport between individuals, and between the teacher and the rest of the group. Work hard to create a healthy and positive learning environment with your teenage learners – one that is characterised by mutual trust and respect. In order for these group norms and values to prevail, we have to make a sustained effort to mould them and uphold them.

The relationship between teenage students and their teacher can be fragile. It takes a long time to build rapport, so tread carefully. Remember that weeks of hard work can be undone in a matter of seconds with a careless word or action.

1. Accept teenagers for who they are

Take students seriously. Accept their views, opinions, preferences or fashion choices. You might not agree with their views, but allow them to be heard. Remember that acceptance is not the same as approval. If you disagree strongly with something a teenage student says, don't be dismissive. Avoid comments such as *That's ridiculous*. Instead say *What makes you think so? That's not how I see it.*

2. Uphold important values

Establish ground rules of respect and tolerance. Work hard to uphold important values and defend them during lessons. Set a personal example yourself with your words and actions. Don't let things slide: be quick to intervene on behalf of a student if they are disrespected by a classmate. Disrespectful words and behaviour towards the teacher should not go unchallenged, either. Do this consistently, firmly and calmly. Let students realise how much it matters to you.

3. Don't make fun of students

Never go for a cheap laugh at a student's expense. Teenagers sometimes do or say clumsy or awkward things during class. Avoid the temptation to get a laugh from the rest of the group by drawing attention to an individual's embarrassment or discomfort. The student in question will hate you for it. And behind their laughter, the others will be wondering if you are going to do the same to them next time.

4. Don't talk about students behind their backs

Light-hearted comments about students who are absent from class should be avoided, even if they are not intended to be malicious. Comments such as *[Student A] isn't here. So that's why it's so quiet today!* or *What's the matter, [Student B]? Are you missing [Student C]?* plant a seed of suspicion and uncertainty in students' minds. Teenagers will start to wonder what the teacher says about them when they are absent.

5. **Explain unpopular decisions**

Tell students what is behind your decision making. For example, if you have promised students a certain activity as a reward for effort or attitude, make sure that they have earned it before granting it. Try to illustrate the connection between actions and consequences, especially when you feel that agreements made between you and the students have not been kept. Give them a chance to respond before making a final decision.

6. **Give them a chance to make amends**

Don't burn your bridges prematurely. It can take teenagers a while to adjust to a new teacher, and there will inevitably be mistakes, misjudgements and misunderstandings. Try to make sure that any unpleasantness is provisional rather than permanent. Help students to turn things around by identifying clear steps they can take to remedy the situation. Give them a chance to make amends, and suspend your judgement until then.

7. **Don't judge them on past behaviour**

Avoid pigeonholing students on the basis of previous mistakes or indiscretions. Our relationship with our teenage students will only be able to develop in a healthy way if we steer it in that direction. Focus on current positives rather than past negatives. Point out examples of positive outcomes or attitudes when you see them. Use phrases such as *That's what I like to see*. There is no need to keep reminding students of things that have gone wrong in the past.

8. **Make yourself available to students**

Get into the habit of scanning the room with your eyes during lessons to see if students want to say something. Move around the room and invite comments and questions. Don't brush students off, wave away their requests, or tell them to *Just get on with it* when they ask a question about classroom tasks. That only increases the likelihood of passive behaviour and quiet resentment. We should be helping teenage students to be more active, and encouraging them to interact with us is one way of doing this.

9. **Challenge counterproductive mindsets**

Challenge students when they make negative judgements about themselves. These are indicative of what is known as a 'fixed mindset'. Focus on individual improvement as a milestone for achievement. Reward effort and attitude, and try to promote a healthier growth mindset by helping students to set *getting better* as their main goal. Support this in the way you evaluate students' work. For more on mindsets, see Dweck C (2006) *Mindset*. Penguin Random House.

10. **Discuss problems honestly**

If tension between you and the students persists, don't ignore it or hope that it will simply go away. Unless tackled, problems in the class can become entrenched and difficult to resolve. Try to get to the bottom of the problem by discussing it with your students openly. Say *I can see that something is bothering you* or *Let me tell you what I think is going on, and you can tell me if I'm right or not*. Such discussions need to be held calmly and diplomatically.

10 ways of dealing with students' names

Make it a priority to learn the names of your teenage students as quickly as you can. Try to learn all the names in the first lesson or two. Managing a new group of teenage students is much easier once you are no longer struggling to match names to faces. Teens also generally respond more positively to teachers who make a noticeable effort to learn their names than to those who do not.

Use names to bring distracted teenagers gently back into the lesson. Teenagers might not always hear our instructions, but they always respond to their names being said. Be mindful of the fact that teenagers are also sensitive about their names. Students will not appreciate it if we seem uninterested in getting their names right, or if we deal with their names in a flippant or jokey way.

1. Get students to make name cards

Begin your first lesson with a new group of students by asking them to make a personalised name card for themselves. Provide paper and pens for this. Tell students to write the name they would like the teacher to use when talking to them in class (not necessarily their full name). Walk around the room as students do this, checking that you can read the names and testing your pronunciation if necessary.

2. Make a seating plan

As students are completing their name cards, quickly write a seating plan in your notebook, showing the name of each student and where they are sitting. Ask students to sit in the same seat for the first few lessons, or until you have learned all the names. Keep your seating plan somewhere you can refer to it easily mid-lesson, as sometimes it is difficult to read the students' name cards from the front of the room. In subsequent lessons, the seating plan can also be used to work out which students are absent.

3. Do activities with the name cards

Use the name cards as a learning tool. If the students do not know each other's names yet, jumble up all the name cards and distribute them to students randomly. Ask them to return their card to its rightful owner. At the end of the first lesson, collect all the name cards. Begin the next lesson by attempting to give each card back to the student it belongs to, perhaps calling on the help of the others in the group.

4. Get students to tell you something about their name

Ask each student to tell you and the class something about their name. Give them options. They can tell you the meaning of their name, how they got it, an anecdote in connection with it, or their feelings about it. This activity can be an effective way of establishing some rapport with students, and is also a good way to help you remember students' names.

5. Get students to suggest mnemonics

As you set about the task of getting to know students, ask them to suggest mnemonic devices that can help you to remember their names. One way of doing this is to ask them to think of an apt English adjective to describe themselves, starting with the same sound/letter as the first letter of their name. This might result in 'tall Tomas' or 'funny Flora', for example.

6. Give students control over their names

Teenage students occasionally have issues in connection with their name. They might not like the way the teacher pronounces it, or may simply wish to be called something else, especially if their classmates, parents and other teachers are all in the habit of calling them by some variation of their name, or even a different name altogether. Respect students' wishes in these situations, as long as it does not make you feel uncomfortable.

7. Be careful with nicknames

We should not automatically assume that it is appropriate for us to use the nicknames that students use for each other. There are occasions when teenagers genuinely feel that their nickname is their real name (see above), but in many instances, teenagers find it overly informal and familiar if the teacher falls idly into the habit of using student nicknames in class. Proceed with caution.

8. Use students' names frequently

The best way to learn names is to use them. Whenever you call on a student or respond to a question or comment, address them by their name. If you get it wrong, apologise and correct yourself. Try to make sure you use every student's name in every class. This helps to bring all the students into the lesson, and increases teenagers' sense of involvement. There are indirect techniques for doing this as well, for example, mentioning students rather than calling on them. For example, you can say *We finished revising Unit 4 last lesson, and as [Student A] remembers, I said we would do something different today.*

9. Check you're using all the names

Invite a colleague who does not know the group to observe you teaching them. Give your observer a blank seating plan, showing the position of students in the room, but not revealing their names. As you teach the class, give your observer the task of adding the students' names to the seating plan as and when he or she hears their names being used. You could also get the observer to indicate whether the name was first mentioned by the teacher (T) or by another student (S). The more student-to-student interaction there is in a lesson, the more we would expect there to be some examples of students referring to or addressing other members of the group by name.

10. Find out which names you're using the most – and the least

As an alternative to the activity described in tip 9 above, set your observer the task of counting how often each student's name is used during the lesson. This can help you to identify which students are getting more than their fair share of attention, and which ones are being overlooked.

10 ways to deal with teenage behaviour problems

It is unusual for there *not* to be some discipline and behaviour problems with teenage students, especially during the first few weeks with a new group. It is natural to expect a few teething troubles as the teacher and students gradually become familiar with each other's personalities and working methods, but issues sometimes persist.

Think about preventing problems from emerging in the first place, as well as developing strategies for how you are going to handle difficulties once they happen.

Be firm and consistent in the way you approach problems with behaviour and discipline and, above all, be calm. Try to take a detached, constructive approach. Remember that the disruptive and disrespectful behaviour of adolescents is usually a result of their immaturity, rather than of any malicious desire to cause offence or to stir up trouble. Be mature in your response to immature behaviour. Don't lash out or go down to their level.

In the vast majority of cases, teens actually prefer – and want – lessons in which there are no behaviour or discipline issues. When discipline and behaviour problems are caused by teenagers' immaturity, the problems are often exacerbated by lacklustre teaching, boring lessons and poor classroom-management decisions. We should try to bear this in mind when dealing with the behaviour problems that we are experiencing. Small changes to our approach coupled with a positive attitude can sometimes have fruitful results.

1. Don't wait for problems to take root

Try to anticipate difficulties and act before problems emerge. Monitor students carefully in class, and investigate potential problem areas when they are still in their formative stage. For example, if two neighbouring students are chatting too much in class, talk to them after the lesson and see if you can resolve the issue in this way first, before taking any further steps, such as asking them to sit apart. Another option is to ask students *Is there anything about the lessons that's bothering you?* Give them the opportunity to answer in writing, anonymously if necessary. This is another effective way to become aware of potential problems and to nip them in the bud.

2. Remain focused

Let students see that your lessons cannot easily be derailed. There is a tendency for teenage students to put new teachers to the test. Clowning around in the first few lessons is often associated with testing the boundaries. Be ready to respond assertively, but be careful not to over-react to boisterous or slack behaviour in the early stages. Respond to poor discipline with calm directions and firm requests, while you stay focused on the lesson. Teenagers are much less likely to misbehave on purpose on a regular basis if they see that the teacher is focused and unflustered.

3. Take control at the start of lessons

A key time to think about discipline issues is between classes. Reflect on your previous lesson with the group. The students saw that you were firm and remained focused on the class, but there were probably some issues that bothered you. At the start of the next lesson, reiterate your expectations and requirements regarding behaviour. Tell them in a calm and assertive way what you *want* to see them do, not what you *don't want* to see them do.

4. **Communicate verbally**

As teenagers' brains grow, there is often an interim stage in which they find it surprisingly hard to read facial expressions. If a student has begun to misbehave, don't rely on body language or facial expressions to signal your dissatisfaction. They might simply miss it. Have a firm, quiet word instead. As ever, use the kind of constructive language that tells the student what they have to do, rather than dwelling on what they're doing wrong.

5. **Model a mature approach**

Teenagers want to be treated like adults, but often do not yet know how to behave in a mature way themselves. Maintain adult-like self-control and self-discipline in your interactions with misbehaving teenage students. Don't be snappy, sarcastic, or sulky. Show them how a mature and responsible adult handles conflict situations. They can – and often do – learn from us.

6. **Withhold rewards**

If teenagers generally enjoy the content of our lessons, they are much less likely to misbehave. Make sure that – as a general rule – your lessons culminate in activities that the students enjoy. When you experience unacceptable behaviour problems in a class, withhold the activities that students had been looking forward to, and explain why you are doing this. This is far more effective in the long run than punishing students with tedious 'retaliatory' tasks or additional disciplinary measures.

7. **Give students a chance to self-correct**

You might find that a generally well-behaved teenager is having a day when they find it hard to control their juvenile impulses. This is especially true of younger teens. Typical signs of this include pestering their neighbour, making 'sound-effect' noises, clicking and spinning their pens, or giggling uncontrollably. If this begins to disrupt your teaching, give the student a face-saving way to self-correct. An effective technique for doing this is to say that you think the student must be thirsty, and, staying calm and focused on the lesson, firmly invite the student to go to the bathroom to have a drink of water. Having the chance to leave and re-enter the classroom (while the teacher calmly carries on teaching) often has the effect of allowing the student to press the reset button on their behaviour. If the problem continues, asking *Are you thirsty?* again acts as an effective reminder.

8. **Chat to your 'problem' student**

When behaviour problems among individuals are chronic or linked to out-of-school or family issues, it can be much harder – even impossible – for the teacher to have a transformative impact. Regular, non-confrontational chats with so-called 'problem' students can, however, be surprisingly effective in adjusting their attitudes towards our lessons. Identify the student you wish to focus on. Ask them to stay behind after class. The student will probably be defensive, or protest that they *didn't do anything*. Chat to the student for a couple of minutes, in L1 if possible. Don't mention behaviour or refer to anything that happened in that day's class. Choose a neutral, everyday topic, such as the previous night's football match. Try to replicate the kind of low-key chat that you might have with a colleague in the staffroom. Repeat this procedure for several lessons in succession, with the same student each time. This kind of non-confrontational, non-judgemental interaction enables you both to see each other in a new light, and can help to re-calibrate the student's attitude and behaviour. It may seem like a lot of effort, but the results can make it worthwhile. Remember, also, that so-called 'problem' students are often influential members of the class: if their behaviour or attitudes begin to change, so does that of others in the group.

9. Use disciplinary meetings constructively

If individual behaviour problems persist, you might need to have a sit-down with the student in question, perhaps with another member of staff or the school head. These meetings are traditionally rather unproductive, often consisting of little more than finger-wagging or the issuing of warnings. Instead, try to get to the bottom of the problem by searching for the underlying beliefs that lie behind discipline and behaviour problems. This can be extremely difficult if students are guarded, defensive, or unwilling to talk, so ask questions and pay attention to how the student responds. *Is it because …?* is an effective way to frame questions with defensive teenagers. Try prompts such as *Is it because you think that you're no good at English? / Is it because you think that you're not going to understand? / Is it because you feel that the others are going to look down on you? / Is it because you feel that the teacher is being unfair?* Expect a lot of *No* answers. Teens might not open up straight away to these prompts, but a long pause from a student after a question can be extremely revealing in these situations.

10. Reflect on your actions and their consequences

Focus on learning from experience. From a behaviour point of view, some strategies will work, and some strategies will not. Take the time to reflect on both. Write down a few thoughts after lessons about which strategies you feel were significant in either a positive or a negative sense. Look for connections between what you did in the lesson and what happened as a result. Think about possible changes and alterations that you could make to your approach, and then note down the results when you apply them in the classroom in subsequent lessons.

> *"Most behaviour problems I've found come from sheer boredom or/and excessive sitting. I think teenagers can be a pain in the neck, yes, but at the same time they keep teachers on their toes. We are forced to create an engaging and participatory learning environment to survive. We also need to be truthful at all times because they smell deception."*
>
> **Elvira Carralero, English teacher, Escuela Oficial de Idiomas de San Javier, Murcia, Spain**

10 ways to get the best out of mixed-ability teen classes

Think beyond language proficiency as a descriptor of 'ability' when working with mixed teenage groups. Look for ways to give all students a foothold in the lesson, by providing varied and flexible tasks that combine both language skills and non-language skills.

Teenagers' preconceptions about their capabilities can be both positively and negatively affected by the way in which language-learning activities are handled in the classroom. Providing students with opportunities to see compelling evidence that they are capable of making progress is the best strategy for sustaining motivation and for helping students in mixed-ability classes to boost their self-esteem and to achieve their goals.

1. Talk about strengths as well as weaknesses

Get students to identify things that they are good at, as well as areas that they need to work on. Include learning attitudes and habits as areas for discussion. Stress the need for getting better across all areas, as well as the potential for learning from each other. Teenagers have a tendency to rank themselves within the group. Try to help students see that they all have their own strengths and weaknesses.

2. Differentiate flexibly

Differentiate language-learning activities, for example, by occasionally producing different versions of texts for students to read, or by offering different ways of responding to language input. Instead of always allocating differentiated tasks to students based on their language level, allow them to choose which option they would like to work on.

3. Use open-ended questions

Give students open-ended questions that allow them to respond to prompts in a number of ways, according to their language level or personal opinion. Look for questions that have no single right answer, and that can be answered in either simple or more complex ways. For example, ask students which one of the following they would choose to give up if they had to, and why: their passport, their mobile phone, or their sense of smell.

4. Provide options and choices

Calibrating the level of language difficulty is not the only way to ensure differentiation. Give students options regarding task type, working modes and item choice. From time to time, provide students with a selection of different task types to choose from. Alternatively, let students decide whether they want to complete tasks individually or in pairs. A third idea is to let students choose which questions out of a set of 10 to answer, for example by asking them to answer *any six questions in any order.*

5. Activate non-cognitive skills

Design language tasks which engage skills that have little or nothing to do with language learning. For example, ask students to work in pairs to identify key words in a poem or short text describing a person or event. Then ask them to compare their selections and create a picture of the person or event by arranging the words they have collected to make an image.

6. Let students have several attempts at tests

Try two-stage testing. When students have completed a short test, tick the correct items but leave the rest uncorrected. Make a note of the scores. Then provide the chance for in-between learning, letting students go back to consult their book or other resources. At the following class, hand the test out again, and give students a second chance to complete it. The final score is the student's average score over two attempts. To ensure students try hard the first time, give the first percentage score slightly more weight than the second one.

7. Encourage co-operation and collaboration

Encourage teenage students to help each other. In the activity described above, encourage students to explain questions to each other at the in-between learning stage. When doing pairwork or groupwork activities, encourage students to work with different partners occasionally, in order to increase the potential for peer-learning and peer-teaching.

8. Make use of L1

If you speak the students' L1, don't be afraid to use it sometimes when setting up tasks, providing explanations, or giving feedback to mixed-ability groups. Using the L1 can clear up uncertainty and help to increase confidence. Occasionally, design communicative tasks in which students use their first language as part of the activity. (See Unit 13 for activities using L1).

9. Welcome gaps in knowledge

Don't be too pleased if students manage do a task with no mistakes: this indicates that it was not difficult enough. Encourage students to set themselves challenges that they can learn from. Help students to be intrigued by what they don't know, rather than getting upset about it. In class, write the statements *I can't do this* and *I can't do this yet* on the board, and ask students to compare them. Get them to unpack the attitude towards learning and ability that are implied in each sentence.

10. Use a whole-person approach

Get students thinking about skills instead of ability. Draw special attention to the importance of non-cognitive skills in learning (such as not giving up, asking for help, taking on challenges, working together, etc.). When evaluating students' progress, take these factors into account. For example, award extra points in tests to reflect how well students have been able to apply such skills. Try to reward learning processes as well as learning outcomes.

10 techniques for developing teenagers' study skills

Teachers sometimes take it for granted that teenagers know how to study, or that they are already skilled at autonomous learning outside the classroom. In fact, teenagers often have a haphazard approach to learning, and in many cases are not consciously aware of what study skills are or how to use them effectively.

Left on their own, teenagers often struggle to make sense of the notes they have written, or they look through the textbook without any awareness of strategies or study-skills techniques. Our job is both to raise their awareness of what effective study skills are, and to provide activities in and out of class that can help teenagers to acquire them.

1. Personalise learning goals

Help students to make a distinction between what they *have to learn*, and what they *would like to learn*. Having personalised learning goals can help teenagers to be more motivated, and also allows them to develop important study skills, such as how to research a topic. At the beginning of a unit, introduce the topic of the unit and ask students to write down three questions that they want to be able to answer about the topic by the end of the unit. Later, get students to look back and see how many of their questions they can now answer. If there are any unanswered questions, discuss ways in which they could find out the answers they need. Support them in their research.

Unit 21

2. Share memory techniques

Write 10 unrelated words on the board and challenge students to memorise them in sequence. Give them two minutes for this task. Then remove the words from the board and ask students to write down all the words in the right order from memory. Check and compare answers. Then ask students what techniques – if any – they used to remember the words. This activity provides a useful opportunity for students to share effective memorising techniques. You can also share your own techniques for doing tasks like this with the class.

3. Help students to remain focused

When it comes to studying out of class, teenagers often struggle to make good use of the time at their disposal, and find themselves easily distracted. One common obstacle is boredom. In class, get students to work in pairs or small groups and ask them to share or come up with constructive ways to stave off boredom in a 45-minute study period at home. Teenagers often have creative and amusing solutions, such as *eating one raisin for every five words learned* or *doing 10 press-ups every 10 minutes*. Again, this activity gives students the opportunity to talk about the obstacles they face when studying, and allows them to share ideas that work for them.

4. Help students not to be distracted by their phones while studying

Ask students if they ever get distracted by their mobile phones when they're trying to study. Suggest some techniques for reducing the likelihood of this happening, for example:

- Switch off the Wi-Fi.
- Activate airplane mode.
- Turn the screen display to black and white.

- Put the phone in another room.
- Switch off the phone and give it to a parent for one hour.

Ask teenagers to discuss the advantages and disadvantages of each method, and to think of any other techniques that might work. For homework, ask students to try out one of the techniques and then report back.

5. Compare note-taking techniques

Prepare a five-minute presentation on the topic of *taking notes*. Tell the students that their task is to listen to the presentation – and to take notes. Your presentation might introduce and demonstrate a few note-taking techniques, such as mind maps, bullet points, word abbreviations, or sketch noting. At the end of the presentation, get students into small groups and ask them to rank the methods that were discussed in the presentation in order of usefulness. Then ask students to look at the notes that they took themselves. Get them to compare the various techniques used by different students in the group, and to discuss which ones seem to have been the most effective for the task.

6. Do collaborative note-taking activities

Get students to work together on a dictogloss task. This activity involves individual note-taking followed by collaborative reconstruction of a text. Find a suitable text and read it aloud at just under normal speed. Get students to take notes. Read the text again, allowing students to add more notes. Then ask students to work in pairs. Get them to write out the complete text. In order to do this, they will have to draw on their notes, their memory, and their working knowledge of how the language works.

7. Work on paraphrasing skills

Many teenage students lack paraphrasing skills when trying to convey the key content of a paragraph that they want to make use of in a presentation or assignment. Often, they simply copy and paste the whole paragraph word-for-word, unaware that this is plagiarism. Practise paraphrasing skills. In class, show students a paragraph of text, and get them to *read, think and write*. First they read the paragraph through carefully, thinking about its content. When they have finished reading, allow them to write down a few key words. Then remove the paragraph from view. Finally, ask students to refer to their notes and write an original paragraph, making use of the information contained in their notes.

8. Ask students to give revision presentations

Get students to prepare short revision presentations on topics or language areas already covered in class. They can do this individually or in pairs. Give the presenters a five-minute slot, in which they play the role of the teacher, presenting information to the class. Allow them to use presentation software for this, or let them create a paper handout if they prefer. This technique gives students useful practice at identifying and communicating key information, and really helps them to grasp the content that they are discussing. It also provides you with the opportunity to provide them with feedback on their teaching materials. The materials produced can also be shared with the rest of the group as a revision aid.

9. Get students to write revision tests for each other

At the end of a unit in the coursebook, give students the task of compiling a short test for another student to complete. Students swap papers and try to complete each other's tests. This can be an interesting way to make revision lessons more engaging for teenage students. Another key advantage of asking students to make practice tests is that it helps them to notice things in the unit that they do and don't understand. It also primes them to anticipate and remember the kinds of questions that they might be asked in the actual test.

10. Test students' predictions

Before asking the first question in a vocabulary test, tell students how many items there are going to be. Then ask them to predict how many points they are going to get, and to write it at the top of the page. Underneath that, ask them to write down how many minutes they spent preparing for the test. Teenagers should be able to draw their own conclusions.

"To avoid frustration on all sides, it's good to accept that not every study method suits every student. To promote intrinsic motivation, have them try out various possibilities and report back what works and why. Experience teaches me that a student is not a machine and that education is firmly based on relationship. While offering tips about ideal study skills, I try to be sensitive to the mood of the moment: what is possible for that student on that day?"

Corinne Bason, Erwachsenenbildung Oberrieden, Switzerland

10 ways to end lessons

Establish routines for the end of the lesson and use them to help nurture a positive learning environment. When teenage students know that there is something to look forward to at the end of the lesson, it can help them to remain focused on their work. The occasional decision to withhold these activities can also be effective when it comes to dealing with behaviour and discipline issues (see Unit 19).

Some end-of-class activities, such as games, quizzes and video clips, are high-intensity, and can be used to finish the lesson in a stirring way. Often, however, teenagers appreciate settling activities, which help them to catch their breath for a moment or two. These settling activities are especially effective if they provide teenagers with a certain amount of freedom to choose what to do.

Whatever you do with teenage students, be sure to end lessons on time. The break is theirs, and they need every second of it.

1. Watch a clip

Teenagers are often keen to share interesting or amusing online video clips with their teacher and with the rest of the class. The end of the lesson is the ideal time to do this, as long as you feel that students have earned this treat. Take steps to make sure that the content of clips is appropriate for the classroom, perhaps by checking them before playing them to the whole class.

2. Play a game

Teenagers enjoy playing competitive games on the board, such as *Blockbusters* (see Unit 33.6). These games provide us with an ideal chance to review recently learnt language and vocabulary in an engaging way. Teens often like to compete in the same teams every lesson, and sometimes keep a running score of the game results from lesson to lesson.

3. Ask a quiz question

Ask students a general knowledge question at the end of the lesson, and give a bonus point to the student who is the first to provide the correct answer. The winner of the bonus point can choose a classroom privilege – such as being the first to leave – or points can be recorded until students have collected enough of them to warrant a grade. Watch TV or follow the local news to find questions that are topical.

4. Set a puzzle or brainteaser

Give teenagers something to think about at the end of the lesson by giving them a brainteaser or puzzle to solve. Encourage students to post their guesses on the group's online page, and reveal the answer at the start of the next class. This is a nice way of connecting the end of one lesson to the start of the next one.

5. Review the online group page

In the last few moments of the lesson, open the group's online page and comment on anything of interest that has been posted there. Face-to-face discussion of your online interactions with the group can help to boost the frequency and quality of student posts.

6. Allocate roles and responsibilities for the next class

Use the end of class to set a purposeful tone for the next lesson. One way to do this is to allocate teenagers certain roles and responsibilities for the next class. This can help them to arrive for the next lesson in a more motivated state of mind. (For more on responsible roles for students, see Unit 14.)

7. Let students start the homework

If there are a few minutes left at the end of the lesson and you are not sure how to fill them, one technique is to tell students they can start to do their homework. A proportion of the students usually get started straight away; others are more reluctant. One of the benefits of starting the homework in class is that it creates unfinished business in teenagers' minds, making it harder for them to forget about it later.

8. Make yourself available

Another way to use spare time at the end of the lesson constructively is to make yourself available to students who have questions or queries. While the rest of the class occupies itself starting (or pretending to start) the homework, indicate that any students who want to talk to you one-to-one can come over to your desk.

9. Let one student be the first to leave

Teenagers usually can't wait to get out of the classroom at the end of the lesson, so turn this to your advantage. Give one student the privilege of leaving the classroom first, either in recognition of good effort during the lesson, or as the prize for answering a quiz question correctly (see point 3). This is the kind of reward that teenagers genuinely appreciate.

10. Talk to the last student in the room

Occasionally, you might find that one student is taking longer than usual to leave the classroom at the end of the lesson. This can be a signal that they would like to chat to you – but only if you initiate it. As you tidy up your desk at the end of the lesson, get into the habit of noticing which student is the last to leave, and say something to them just before they reach the door. It is surprising how often they then stop to chat.

"I make a point of thanking my students at the end of each lesson. It's important for me to remember that I can learn a lot from them, too, and that co-operation is essential."

Desislava Slavova, Bulgaria

Developing skills

The units in the following section focus mainly on activities and techniques for developing listening, speaking, reading and writing skills with teenage students, both inside and outside the classroom. The ideas and tips in this section assume that, for the most part, teenage students are not likely to be enthusiastic participants in classroom activities that focus on skills development. That is not necessarily a problem, as long as the activities of the lesson are clear, manageable, and can be followed by the students. There is often a feeling that there is something missing, though, and that the students would learn faster and more effectively if they didn't find it all such a drag. So in addition to asking ourselves: *Is this an effective activity?* when practising skills in class, it is also worth asking: *Could I make it any more engaging?*

One effective way to encourage teenage students to take part more actively in skills-development activities is to appeal to their sense of curiosity by giving tasks an element of the unexpected – which is what many of the ideas in this section attempt to do. The classroom also provides an ideal setting for collaborative awareness-raising work on skills development. Activities that get teenage students working together not only provide much-needed variety, they are also more likely to lead to language-learning outcomes that are more memorable – and therefore more valuable. There are real benefits to be had, too, in focusing on micro-skills (for example, looking at drafting skills within the context of writing) but teenagers are prone to lose interest, especially if they feel that the teacher is asking them to do too much extra work, or to repeat things again and again. The units in this section look at these areas, among others.

Some of the tips and ideas in this section look at ways of helping teenage students to pay attention to the language around them when they are out of the classroom, harnessing their curiosity about the English-speaking world, and helping them to engage more conscientiously with the English that they encounter in the course of their everyday lives.

There is also a unit that addresses critical thinking, suggesting ways that it is possible to use the texts, tasks and activities of the English lesson to help teenagers hone their critical-thinking skills.

In many cases, coursebook activities and materials with a skills focus are designed to provide exam practice for students, so teenagers often view them as something of a chore. A further aim of the units in this section is therefore to showcase ways in which skills-focused exam practice can be made more engaging and appealing for teenage students with the help of collaborative working methods and unconventional tasks.

When it comes to providing feedback to teenage learners on skills development, a less-is-more approach is taken, with the emphasis on providing focused, manageable feedback, rather than overloading students with an exhaustive inventory of areas to work on.

10 ways to help teenagers become confident listeners

Unit 23

Many teenagers associate listening with assessment, perhaps because so many of the listening tasks done in the classroom mirror the format of the listening component of language exams. As a result, many teens are reluctant listeners and often approach practice activities with a fair amount of anxiety.

Although listening is a receptive skill, it does not need to be practised in a passive and reactive way. There is more we can do with listening in the teenage classroom than testing comprehension. By experimenting with different types of audio input, offering a variety of task types and giving students more control over the listening process, it is often possible to help teenage students become more confident listeners.

1. Do live monologues

Planned, unscripted monologues by the teacher can be an excellent and confidence-boosting source of authentic listening material for students. Get into the habit of giving students a focused listening task based on a short anecdote or story that you deliver yourself. Plan what you are going to do: come up with questions to ask students beforehand, and think about the general content of what you are going to say. The monologue should not be scripted, however: that's what will make it an authentic listening task. Bear in mind that your students are already used to listening to you speak in class and your voice is therefore familiar and easily understood, especially if you can regulate your speech effectively.

2. Use pre-listening tasks to build confidence

Don't simply pre-teach useful vocabulary in the pre-listening phase of a task. Priming teenagers to notice specific vocabulary items can actually be counterproductive: students begin the task with a narrow focus, often waiting to hear certain specific words rather than listening more freely. A better way to give students confidence is to discuss the general topic of the recording first. Elicit relevant background information and find out what students know about the topic already. When it comes to students feeling confident about listening, being able to demonstrate that they already know something about the context is arguably more beneficial than being fed a handful of words by the teacher.

3. Keep it short

Save longer audio texts for exam practice. If you're trying to boost students' confidence in listening, keep it short. Thirty seconds is enough. Anything longer than a minute is likely to sap the confidence of some students in the group.

4. Do short dictations

Make a habit of giving students short dictations – one or two sentences only – every lesson. One dictation sentence might be *What did you have for breakfast?* First ask students to count how many words you say. (If you are using connected speech, this might not be obvious.) Confirm the correct answer – in this case, six words. Then repeat the dictation, asking students to write down exactly what you say.

5. Try open-ended listening

Comprehension questions are fine for exam practice, but if students lack confidence, they can have a restricting effect. Instead of setting the agenda for listening, allow students to construct the content as they listen. Play a short recording, then give students a chance to confer in pairs. Then ask students *What was that about?* or *What can you tell me about what we just heard?* Allow students to listen to the recording several times.

6. Do collaborative listening

Get students into pairs for listening tasks, or into groups of three or four. This is an excellent way to take the pressure off, and often leads directly to increased confidence. Teenagers are likely to confer during listening tasks anyway, so incorporate it into task design. A further advantage of collaborative listening is that it mirrors many real-life listening situations, in which a group of people interpret a spoken message together.

7. Give students the controls

Give students access to a short recording on their phones. One way to do this is to set up a class group on an instant messaging platform (such as WhatsApp) and to post the audio clip there. Get students into groups of three or four. One student controls the playback, pausing and re-playing as often as the others indicate. Students work collaboratively to interpret the content of the clip, or to answer questions about it.

8. Use student recordings

Teenagers are generally intrigued to listen to recordings made by people in their peer group, especially if the speakers are students at their school. Ask students in a more senior class to give you permission to make an audio recording of them doing a communicative speaking activity. Use this as the basis for a listening task with a more junior group of students in the same school.

9. Use recordings of people with the same L1 as your students

Look online for audio and video clips in English made by speakers from your students' country. It is usually easier to understand someone speaking English who has the same first language as you. Proficient or skilled speakers can also serve as positive role models for your students, as can other teachers in the school.

10. Find speakers of different ages

Teenagers get weary of listening to the carefully modulated language of adult speakers. Experiment by occasionally using authentic clips of young children and older people – who usually speak more slowly, and can therefore be more easily understood.

10 ways to exploit out-of-class listening opportunities

Teenagers rarely need to be told to start listening to English out of class; in many cases they are already exposed to plenty of spoken English as they go about their daily lives and in their free-time viewing. We can, however, help them to become better at noticing the spoken language that they hear – and to pay attention to the language-learning opportunities it offers.

Some of the activities below involve noticing the English that is already around us; others direct students to online and recorded sources of spoken language in an engaging and interactive way.

1. Capture the English they hear in public

Get students to engage with the English they hear around them. One way to do this is to give students the task of recording any announcements they hear in English outside class. In large cities, public transport announcements at airports, stations or on buses are often repeated in English. Play students' recordings in class and get the rest of the class to say where they think the announcement was recorded and what they think it means.

2. Watch TV shows again

Teenage students often watch a lot of TV programmes and films in their free time, either dubbed into L1 or in English with subtitles. Once they have finished an episode, encourage them to watch it again the next day, this time in English without subtitles. Ask them to make a note of any new language that they noticed. This provides a good opportunity for extensive listening.

3. Watch short clips to practise intensive listening

As an out-of-class task, ask students to select a 30-second clip from a favourite TV series or movie. They can choose any scene or segment from the recording that they have just watched. First, ask them to watch their selected clip in English with the subtitles switched off or covered up. Afterwards, get them to watch the clip again, this time with subtitles turned on. As they watch, ask them to notice any differences between the subtitled script and what was actually spoken.

4. Listen to song lyrics

When hearing a song for the first time, students try to make a note of the song's refrain or chorus. This will be repeated throughout the song, so students will have several chances to hear it. Get them to write down exactly what they think the words of the chorus are, and ask them to check by looking for the lyrics online afterwards. As a follow-up, ask students to write down song lyrics by watching clips on YouTube out of class. They can check their transcriptions afterwards by searching for the lyrics online or by watching a subtitled version of the song on YouTube.

5. Eavesdrop

Encourage students to listen in on any conversations they hear around them in English, and – if appropriate – to join in. For example, they might overhear English-speaking tourists trying to work out directions or attempting to decipher a train timetable, in which case providing the required information would be both appropriate and helpful. In class, get students to report back on any English conversations they heard.

6. Share trailers

Trailers and teasers for TV shows and movies are short, engaging, and full of interesting language. Ask students to find an online trailer for a movie or TV show that they have seen and to post the link to the class's online group. The other students watch each chosen trailer and decide which one they are most interested in following up.

7. Do 'today I learned' challenges

Ask students to choose a topic or subject matter that they are interested in and look for online videos made by other people who are also interested in the topic. They might find a short tutorial film connected to the topic, or it could be a video report. Students watch the video and write down two or three things that they learned from it.

8. Explore podcasts

Ask students to calculate how much dead time they have each day, i.e. time when they are not engaged in any particular activity. One example might be the time spent sitting on the bus each day. Ask students what they do to kill time in these situations, and – with students whose English proficiency is already quite high – discuss the possibility of listening to podcasts. Then give students the out-of-class task of exploring some of the available English-language podcasts on topics that they are interested in. Invite them to try out two or three such podcasts, and to report back on which one they found most interesting and why.

9. Have a voice-memo conversation

Teenagers tend to be prolific users of instant messaging programs, many of which include voice-memo functionality. Encourage students to have an online conversation in English with one of their friends, made up entirely of voice memos.

10. Transcribe a voice memo

As an alternative to the idea above, invite students to write down the content of a voice memo message sent to them by one of their friends, or by the teacher.

10 techniques for improving speaking in roleplays and dialogues

We spend a lot of time in class practising the type of speaking tasks that often feature in spoken exams (roleplays, dialogues, interviews, etc.) In these tasks, students are encouraged to be chatty and talkative in their interactions with their partner. In similar real-life situations, however, teenagers are usually *not* particularly chatty and expansive – especially when talking to adults.

It can also be challenging for teenagers to cope with the pressure of a speaking-exam situation, where the fear of losing face is especially high. The fact that there is not much time to think or collect ideas makes it even more stressful. This pressure can make already self-conscious teenagers feel even more anxious, as they search for language and ideas while trying to stay calm and collected.

Acknowledging these challenges at the practice stage can help provide nervous teenagers with the language tools, ideas and confidence that they need.

1. Practise in L1 first

Try doing a roleplay in the students' first language before doing it in English. This helps teenagers to develop the interactive and interpersonal skills that the task requires. It also helps them to notice the kind of language that is appropriate and useful for the task, which they can then look for in English.

2. Talk about real-life experiences

Teenagers have not always had real-life experience of the situations that crop up in roleplays, for example booking a hotel room or asking for directions in a foreign city. Talk about these situations in class, eliciting what people usually say and do when they find themselves in these situations.

3. Use pocket-phrases and fillers

In Q&A interview tasks, give students pocket-phrases – phrases written on small pieces of paper to be read and pocketed before the activity begins – and fillers, which they can use when they are lost for words or nervous, for example, *Let me think about that for a minute* or *I guess my answer to that question would be ….* This enables students to buy a bit of time, and also gives them the confidence that comes from using a phrase they know is correct.

4. Comment on the question before answering it

In oral exams, questions are not just questions: they're also invitations to speak. Teenagers tend to be in a rush to answer the question – often with just a one-word answer – and struggle to demonstrate fluency. One way around this is to practise commenting on the question before answering it, for example:

- *That's an interesting question.*
- *This isn't really one of my favourite topics, but …*
- *When I think about this topic the first thing that springs to mind is …*
- *Different people have different opinions on this question. Personally, I think …*

5. Explore different ways of saying *I don't know*

Teenagers dread being asked a question they have no idea how to answer: it's the ultimate exam embarrassment. Explain that it is perfectly acceptable not to have an opinion about a question, as long as we can express that. The examiner is not interested in their opinion, after all, but just wants to hear some English. Explore different ways of saying *I don't know*, for example:

- *That's something I've never really thought about.*
- *I wouldn't know how to answer this question in my first language.*
- *I'm not a hundred per cent sure what you are asking with this question.*
- *I've never been asked this question before, so I'm not sure how to answer it.*

In most cases, this will lead to the question being rephrased or modified by the examiner.

6. Ask your partner what he or she thinks

In paired tasks, where students have to discuss a topic together or make a decision about something, teenagers often compete with each other instead of helping each other out. For example, they sometimes think that they should speak more than their partner in order to do well, which can lead to interruptions. A good way to develop interactive communication skills is to encourage students to begin by asking their partner for their opinion.

7. Practise non-verbal communication and phatic responses

Teenagers are not usually very good at signalling that they are following a conversation – or even paying attention. In roleplays and discussions, explain to students that it's important to use non-verbal responses when listening – for example, smiling, nodding, and looking at the speaker. Teenagers often do not know how to react to their partner's utterances, either. Practise using phatic responses that demonstrate empathy or sympathy, for example, *Really? / How awful! / What a nightmare! / Are you serious?* etc.

8. Use speed-dating techniques to energise practice

Teenagers can find speaking practice tasks repetitive and boring, especially if they are working with the same partner. Mix things up occasionally by using speed-dating techniques. Ask students to stand facing each other in two concentric circles. Begin the speaking task. After a few minutes, get the outer circle to rotate, giving each student a new partner.

9. Film it on your phone

When students are practising in pairs, occasionally get them to film their discussion on their mobile phones. This is a simple way to motivate teenagers, but also has the added advantage of giving them a chance to watch themselves speaking. Very often, this makes them more demanding of themselves, leading to multiple recordings – and more practice.

10. Get feedback from a buddy

Teenagers enjoy being given the role of personal coach or adviser. They also value the advice of their peers. Put two pairs together to form a buddy group. While one pair practises their speaking task, the other pair listens and takes notes. They might comment on things like:

- turn-taking
- length of responses
- whether ideas and opinions were illustrated with examples
- range of vocabulary
- accuracy of grammar
- clarity of pronunciation.

Afterwards, they give constructive feedback and advice. Then the students swap roles.

Unit 25

"As I enjoy using technologies in the classroom I decided to start recording my students' roleplays and then post them in Edmodo just for sharing. It turned out that those videos soon became a tool for self-correction as the students started to watch them with a more analytical purpose. I was thrilled!"

Cristina Silva, EFL teacher, Porto, Portugal

10 techniques for managing long turns in speaking

The task of speaking about a topic for an extended period can be very daunting for teenage students. Many students feel that they are incapable of speaking on their own on any topic for up to a minute, and the fear of losing face can make them reluctant to practise in front of others.

The following techniques are designed to be both manageable and enjoyable. The aim is to give students confidence in themselves by providing useful language and effective strategies for handling individual long turns in speaking. In addition to tips about language, the practice activities below also focus on achieving incremental improvement through collaborative preparation and practice, embracing the power of repetition, and learning how to handle prompts and questions flexibly and imaginatively when speaking.

1. Build a collection of opening phrases

Teach students a variety of general introductory phrases that they can use when beginning to talk about a topic, such as *This is an interesting topic and everyone has something to say about it …* or *When I think about this topic the first thing that comes to mind is …* Having a set of ready-made phrases up their sleeve really helps students to overcome their initial nerves, and enables them to begin brightly.

2. Talk about your grandmother

Help students find a solid, personal context for speaking. When students are not sure how to develop the topic they have been given, get them to begin by saying *My grandmother always says …* This simple technique works for any topic and turns a short answer such as *Fast food is not very healthy* into something more complex and interesting: *My grandmother always says fast food is not very healthy.* This also frees the imagination, giving teenagers an immediate idea of how to continue. Point out that they do not have to talk about their real grandmother, or even to tell the truth.

3. Talk about when you were nine

This is a useful technique to give students ideas for connecting the past and present when speaking. Whatever the topic, tell students to begin with the phrase *When I was nine.* As with the previous (grandmother) idea, this technique provides students with both language and context, and eases the path forward, for example, *When I was nine I ate a lot of sweets, but now I eat more healthy food.*

4. Don't worry about the picture

The materials for individual long turns usually include a picture or two, designed to help students get ideas for things to say about the topic. The pictures can actually create more problems than they solve, as many teenagers mistakenly think that they are supposed to describe the picture in detail, and then become stressed if they get a 'bad' picture. Tell students not to worry about describing the picture in detail. Encourage them to use phrases such as *This picture reminds me of …*, which can help them to move their attention away from the confines of the picture to the topic itself.

5. Stop when you've finished

The most embarrassing part of an individual long turn for teenagers is reaching the point when they having nothing left to say – and do not know what to do. Encourage them to stop decisively when they have finished. Teach students assertive, face-saving phrases for indicating that they have finished, such as *And that's all I have to say about this particular topic*, allowing them to bring the monologue to a clean halt rather than have it sputter and run out of gas in a series of *ummms* and *uhhhhs*.

6. Build a chain

Use collaborative, whole-group activities to build discourse-management skills. Introduce a topic and ask Student A to say the first sentence. Then ask Student B to repeat that sentence and to add a second sentence to continue the monologue. Student C repeats the first two sentences, and continues by adding a third, and so on. Once you have six sentences, stop and ask the whole group to repeat the monologue. Finally, get students to try to find ways to improve it.

On the topic of using mobile phones in public, a chain might be developed in the following way:

Student A: Every time I go on the bus, there are people talking on their phones.

Student B: Every time I go on the bus, there are people talking on their phones. Sometimes the conversations are loud and stupid.

Student C: Every time I go on the bus, there are people talking on their phones. Sometimes the conversations are loud and stupid. But sometimes it's funny.

Student D: Every time I go on the bus, there are people talking on their phones. Sometimes the conversations are loud and stupid. But sometimes it's funny. Yesterday I heard this really angry guy.

Student E: Every time I go on the bus, there are people talking on their phones. Sometimes the conversations are loud and stupid. But sometimes it's funny. Yesterday I heard this really angry guy. He was shouting at someone about a baseball cap.

Student F: Every time I go on the bus, there are people talking on their phones. Sometimes the conversations are loud and stupid. But sometimes it's funny. Yesterday I heard this really angry guy. He was shouting at someone about a baseball cap. He said his friend had borrowed it and hadn't given it back.

7. Try it again

Nerves and self-consciousness are constant companions for teenagers when they are doing long turns. Repetition really helps. When a student has finished practising an individual long turn, ask them if they are satisfied with it. Teenagers often say things like *That was terrible* or *I had no idea what to say*. Instead of offering corrections, simply smile and say *OK, would you like to try that again?* There is usually a significant improvement the second time, which the students themselves are also able to notice.

8. Roll the dice

Practice and repetition can get tedious, so look for ways to make it more interesting. One way to do this is to get students into pairs and give them a dice. Each student rolls the dice and has to say a certain number of sentences about the topic based on the number rolled. If, for example, the student rolls a four, he or she must produce four sentences about the topic.

9. Double up

Get two students to give a single monologue, taking turns to speak as if they were a single person. This allows teenagers to come to each other's rescue if one of them dries up, and reduces the anxiety associated with speaking for a long time individually. Afterwards, get them to repeat their monologue, first as a pair and then individually.

10. Play against the clock

In this quick-fire game, students have to talk about a topic for as long as they can, but are not allowed to hesitate, repeat themselves, or go off-topic. Appoint a timekeeper and start the stopwatch when the first student begins to speak. As soon as there is a hesitation, repetition or digression, the clock is paused and the role of speaker moves to the next student, who continues to discuss the topic as the stopwatch starts again. The winner of the activity is the person who is speaking when the stopwatch eventually reaches 60 seconds. The teacher can be the adjudicator, or the responsibility can be shared with the rest of the class.

Unit 26

"In managing long turns (monologues) in speaking for beginner learners, I normally provide a basic template which includes general yet structured phrases like 'In my opinion...', 'My reasons are..' and 'For example...'. For advanced learners, I challenge them to use some preselected low frequency words in their monologues."

Mardiana Idris, English Language Lecturer, Kolej Matrikulasi Teknikal Johor, Malaysia

10 ways to motivate teenage students to read

Teenage students often associate reading with difficult and tedious classroom activities. As a result, they are often reluctant to read. The more students read, however, the easier reading becomes. Our first aim should be to help students get going; with time we can then help them to develop the habit of reading, which ultimately becomes self-sustaining.

Before we begin to read texts with students in class, we have to think about activating some of the language and vocabulary contained in the text. This in itself is not necessarily going to fire teenagers up, though. A more important aim is to spark their curiosity, and to create the desire to read.

1. Offer options and choices

If possible, provide a selection of texts for students to choose from. Being able to choose what to read from a menu of options gives teenagers a sense of agency, and has a slight but significant impact on their subsequent motivation to read.

2. Make use of audio and video

Play students a clip of an audio or video recording of the text you are about to read as a way of getting their attention and increasing their interest in the text to follow. Ask students context questions and ask them to guess what is happening or to speculate about who they think the characters are.

3. Do quizzes with covers

Do activities with books that do not involve any reading. Show students the covers of several books or graded readers and ask them multiple-choice questions about the books. Students are not expected to know the answers, but they have to guess. The cover might help them. You can try this as using a game-show format, perhaps along the lines of *Who Wants to be a Millionaire?*, in which case, contestants have the option of 'phoning' a friend, asking the audience, or having two incorrect answers eliminated. These activities are especially useful if you are trying to get your teenage students to do more extensive reading outside class. The activity is in itself enjoyable and worthwhile as a language task, and it has the added advantage of getting students curious about the books featured in the quiz.

4. Get students to make predictions from illustrations

Show students an illustration from a book or reading text. Ask them to answer a series of questions about the people and events depicted.

5. Start with a sample sentence

On the board as a preliminary task, display a single sentence from a text. Choose a sentence that is fairly ambiguous, and that leaves space for plenty of speculation, for example, *If I do my job properly, thousands of other people have more fun. It's brilliant!'**. Ask students questions about the sentence, such as *Who do you think is speaking? What do you think her job involves?* Get students to make imaginative predictions. This often has the effect of sparking teenagers' curiosity about the text in question, making them more interested in reading it.

*In this case, the job in question is a video-game tester.

6. Don't ask them to read out loud

Reading out loud is difficult and embarrassing for many teenagers, who can become very self-conscious. It is also difficult to process the information contained in a text while reading it out loud. Teenage students will be much less motivated to do reading activities in class if the teacher is in the habit of asking them to read passages aloud.

7. Do jigsaw-reading tasks

Combine reading with other skills to make it more engaging and communicative. Get into the habit of doing jigsaw-reading tasks with students. Break a text into three sections. Get the students into groups of three. Give each student in the group a different section of the text to read. In order to answer questions about the text, they will have to tell each other the relevant information contained in their section of the text.

8. Play with metaphors

Find a metaphor or a piece of highly descriptive language in a text that you would like the students to read. Use this as the basis for a picture description. For example, you could ask them to draw *a huge white turnip with vast black eyes on a never-ending neck*. When students have completed their drawings, ask them to make sense of this scenario and to share their ideas. Announce that the incident is taken from a famous book. Show them the passage in context*. You now have the students' attention, and will find that they will be motivated to do subsequent reading activities based on this text.

In the middle of the night she woke up dreaming of huge white heads like turnips, that came trailing after her, at the end of interminable necks, and with vast black eyes. But being a sensible woman, she subdued her terrors and turned over and went to sleep again.

* From *The Invisible Man* by HG Wells

Unit 27

9. Challenge students to spot mistakes

When doing a whole-class extensive reading project, do regular chapter checks to make sure that all the students are keeping up with the reading. After each chapter, ask one or two students in the group to write a short summary. Tell them to include at least one factual inaccuracy or mistake in their summary of the chapter. Share the summary with the whole class, and ask everyone to find the factual mistakes. This activity allows you to see which students have really read the chapter.

10. Find time in class for extensive reading

Dedicate time in class to reading extensively. This is also known as *drop everything and read*. Let students get out whatever book they are reading and read it in class for five to 10 minutes. This is an extremely effective way to demonstrate how much we value reading. If individual reading is always relegated to out-of-class time, students are likely to draw the conclusion that it cannot be that important. Students are also more likely to continue reading outside class if they have begun reading in the lesson.

10 strategies for handling reading comprehension tasks

We often give our teenage students the useful but sometimes uninspiring task of doing reading comprehension activities for exam preparation. It takes practice for students to become confident at doing these tasks, even if we supply them with useful reading strategies. Classroom time can be spent putting these strategies into practice in freestanding activities, helping students to acquire a better sense of how to apply them in exam conditions.

1. Predict the answers before reading the questions

When the task requires students to answer questions by finding the information in the text, first show them the questions only, and ask them to come up with possible answers before they have seen the text. This can help them to become better at paying close attention to questions, and reduces the likelihood of their getting distracted by irrelevant information once they start reading.

2. Show students the first sentence of each paragraph

Teenagers can initially be reluctant to plough their way through an entire reading text, so first show them the opening sentence of each paragraph in the text (in the right order). Ask them to make as many predictions as they can about what they think the text is about and to compare predictions. Skim-reading a full text by looking at the first sentence in each paragraph is often a very good way to get a sense of the writer's key points, and this technique helps students to get into the habit of doing this.

3. Eliminate the obviously incorrect answers

In multiple-choice reading comprehensions tasks, instead of immediately asking the students to identify the correct answers, do a preliminary activity in which you ask students to choose one answer option for each question that they are sure is definitely *not* the correct answer. This helps students to develop a process-of-elimination approach to tackling multiple-choice questions.

4. Turn multiple-choice questions into game-show quizzes

Give each student the same amount of virtual money to play with. As they come to each question in a set of multiple-choice reading-comprehension items, ask them to decide how much of their money they wish to bet on each of their answers being correct. Check the answers after each question. If their answer was correct, students win whatever they staked on the question (for example, if they staked £60 and got the answer right, they win their money back plus £60); if their answer was incorrect, they lose their stake. As you go through the answers, get students to calculate their winnings and losses after each question.

5. Get students to micro-blog the content of each paragraph

Help teenage students to become more skilled at gleaning important information in texts by asking them to micro-paraphrase the key content of each paragraph in 140 characters or fewer.

6. Use arrowslit texts to help students to skim

Cover up or block most of the text that the students are going to read, leaving only a thin vertical column of text visible in the middle of the page, containing three or four words per line. Ask students to answer gist questions about the content of the text and the text type based on what they can see. Then show students the entire text, and allow them to modify their guesses.

7. Ask students for T/F proof

When answering true-or-false reading comprehension questions, teenagers sometimes rely on their general knowledge or gut instinct, and do not always have the patience to go back to the text to double-check their answers. Ask them to find proof or evidence in the text that their true/false answer is correct. When checking answers, say *Who can prove it?* after each answer, and encourage students to find relevant words in the text that confirm what the correct answer is.

8. Get students to guess new words from context

Show students a new word in a complete sentence and get them to guess its meaning from the context. Ask them to identify the part of speech they think the word is, and to provide a synonym for the word. Encourage students to do this even if they say that they have no idea. Using syntactic clues and sentence context when guessing the meaning of new words are important reading comprehension skills, and they can be developed in this way.

9. Practise guessing what pronouns stand for

Give students sentences containing pronouns, for example, *It's been causing me problems for ages* and *These are popular with children in the school.* Ask students to rewrite the sentences in as many ways as they can, replacing the pronouns (in these examples *it* and *these*) with nouns that fit. Then show students the sentences in context, and ask them to say which nouns the pronouns actually refer to. This activity helps students to become better at noticing whether sentences fit well into gaps in texts.

10. Ask students to make 'sandwich predictions'

Give students a sentence out of context; for example, *This was surprising, but not as surprising as what happened next.* Get them to notice the reference markers in the sentence (*this* and *what happened next*). Now ask them to sandwich the sentence by writing two more sentences – one before and one after – that fit grammatically and cohesively. Then compare their sentences with the actual text from which the sentence is taken (see below). This is another effective way to help students become better at noticing whether sentences fit into gaps in a text or not.

At eight o'clock she called Carla, as promised, but there was no answer. This was surprising, but not as surprising as what happened next. She felt a gentle tap on her shoulder and turned around to see Carla standing right behind her.

The same technique can be used with sentences in which the reference markers are not quite so clearly signposted, requiring students to think carefully about what might precede and follow the given sentence, in both a narrative and a grammatical sense. See the examples below:

- *She decided to order a lemonade this time, though.*
- *He looked in his bag to make sure.*
- *The street was still empty.*

10 techniques to help teenagers plan, draft and revise their writing

Teenagers understand the benefits of planning, drafting and revising their writing – they would just rather not do it. Many teenagers tend to jump into their writing without a clear plan, and then simply hope for the best. Once they have finished a piece of writing, teenagers are often reluctant to make any further changes or improvements to it, especially if it involves more work. It can be especially hard to convince teenage students of the benefit of writing a second draft, or of revising their finished work. Given the choice between 'making it better' and 'being finished', they tend to value the latter more highly.

It therefore makes sense to use techniques that do not ask teenagers to spend extra time or to do more work on their writing. The techniques below are all designed to focus on aspects of planning, drafting and revising in isolation, turning them into freestanding tasks in themselves. The benefit of this approach is that it raises awareness of effective planning, drafting and revising techniques without burdening students with additional work.

Tip: Keep examples of written work produced by your students; they can be turned into sample texts for many of the activities below.

1. Turn a finished composition into a plan

Give students a finished composition to read in class. Go through it together and draw their attention to the paragraph content, the sequencing of ideas, and the examples used by the writer to illustrate key ideas. Then give them the task of creating the writer's plan.

2. Ask them to submit a plan only

Ask students to write a detailed plan for an essay topic, and to submit that as their assignment. They do not have to write the actual essay, only the plan. Grade or evaluate the plans they submit. This is an effective way to motivate students to give their full attention to the task of planning, because the fact that they do not have to write the essay means that the planning phase is no longer tiresome extra work.

3. Develop a plan from a mind map

Mind maps can be effective planning tools, but many teenagers are reluctant to spend time and energy creating them. Demonstrate the effectiveness of mind maps by giving students a completed mind map on a topic and asking them to use it as the basis for planning and structuring the key ideas in a composition. Again, do not ask students to write the composition itself, only to create a detailed plan based on the mind map.

4. Demonstrate free-writing techniques

Teenagers often find it hard to get started with their writing – even if they have a plan to guide them. Help them to overcome this block by asking them to do a freewriting activity. Give students a topic, a plan, and a time limit of five minutes. Start the clock and ask students to write as much as they can, as quickly as they can. Tell them not to worry about accuracy and structure, and not to stop to re-read what they have written. The idea is simply to get words on the page – whatever they might be. After five minutes, get students into groups and ask them to compare what they wrote. This activity not only gives students impetus, it also helps them to get additional ideas.

5. **Write a first draft from a plan**

Give students a completed essay plan on a topic you have been covering in class. Invite them to look at the plan and to add any additional ideas or points that occur to them. Now ask them to write a quick first draft of the composition. Explain that their writing does not have to be polished or perfect – it's just a first draft. When they have finished, collect the students' work but do not grade it or evaluate it.

6. **Comment on your partner's draft**

Do this activity in the lesson following the activity described in point 5 above. First, put students into pairs. Then give them back their first drafts from the previous lesson. Ask students to exchange papers and to read their partner's first draft, writing comments, suggestions and questions in the margins. When they have finished, students swap papers again and read and discuss the comments made.

7. **Compare two drafts**

Give students uncorrected copies of a first and a second draft of a student assignment. Students work in pairs or small groups. Ask them to identify which was the first draft and which was the second draft. Then ask students to list the ways in which the second draft is stronger, providing concrete examples from the texts to illustrate their observations. Compare and discuss the students' ideas. Point out that the improvements of the second draft would not have been possible if there had not been a first draft.

8. **Work with skeleton texts**

When students are practising writing for-and-against essays, give them a skeleton structure containing four paragraph starters: 1) the first sentence of an introductory paragraph, 2) the first sentence of a *pro* paragraph, 3) the first sentence of a *contra* paragraph, and 4) the first sentence of a concluding paragraph. Allow them to use this as a template for their writing.

9. **Jigsaw a finished draft**

Put students into pairs or small groups. Give each group a hard copy of a first draft of an essay, cut up into separate paragraph pieces. First, ask students to arrange the paragraphs into the best order. Then ask them to underline something in each paragraph that could be changed or improved.

10. **Upgrade the vocabulary of finished drafts**

Give students a completed first draft of a piece of writing to look at. Choose a piece in which the writer's lexical choices are repetitive or unimaginative (for example, it contains multiple instances of words like *very interesting, very good* or *very important*). Ask students to upgrade the vocabulary of the text by replacing some of these words with more imaginative alternatives (such as *fascinating, excellent* or *essential*).

10 motivating writing activities for teenagers

Teenage students are not generally too enthusiastic about writing, especially if it's done with pen and paper. They often associate it with doing tests or getting grades, and so it sometimes has negative associations for them. They can also find the act of writing itself slow, tedious and slightly old-fashioned.

Tasks that contain an element of the unexpected often appeal to teens, so try to add a creative twist to traditional tasks. It is also worth making simple changes to the logistics of writing tasks. For example, some of the activities below simply offer an alternative to pen-and-paper modes of writing, which in many cases can be surprisingly motivating for teens. Other activities look at alternatives to word limits for writing tasks.

1. Unusual constraints

Make mundane writing activities more interesting for teenagers by incorporating additional constraints and arbitrary requirements. There is something about a seemingly pointless challenge that many teenagers cannot resist. If the students' task is to write a 120–140 word email to a friend to ask for their advice about finding a summer job, don't expect them to be too eager to get started. Add extra challenges to the task to get students more interested, such as *Write precisely 123 words*, or *Use six different 'colour' words in the email* (or even both).

2. Random phrases

In mixed-ability groups, set students the optional extra challenge of using a particular phrase or expression. Give them an unusual phrase that has absolutely nothing to do with the topic of the activity (for example, 'a warm glass of Sri Lankan mango juice') and ask them to include it in their writing in such a way that it appears natural. This requires a bit of ingenuity on the part of the students, but the challenge is optional, so if they prefer, students can simply complete the activity without using the random phrase.

3. Time limits for writing

Try setting time limits as an alternative to word limits for writing tasks. This is particularly effective in mixed-ability groups, where meeting word limits is easy for some students and difficult for others. Set a time limit for a flexible, open-ended writing task, allowing different students to produce different amounts of writing and still answer the question. Set a timer and ask the students to write until the time is up.

4. Homework selfie

Ask students to send you a selfie of themselves at home with their completed homework clearly visible in the picture. Award a prize or classroom privilege to whoever sends the most creative photograph. This is not an activity so much as an incentive designed to motivate students to do their written homework at home, *not* in the corridor outside the classroom door five minutes before the lesson begins on the day that the work is due – a common phenomenon among teenage students.

5. Convert to QR code

If students are interested in technology, come up with interesting digital-delivery options for handing in written work. For example, occasionally tell students they can use a QR code generator program, such as qr-code-generator.com to convert their written work into a QR code, which they can print and hand in to the teacher. The written text only reveals itself when the teacher uses a QR code reader on their phone to convert it back into text. (If your phone doesn't have a QR code reader already installed on it, you can easily download one for free.) Many teenagers enjoy the novelty of this technique, especially if we are also able to take the time to give our written feedback to the students in QR-code format, as well.

6. Creative problem solving

Transform revision of vocabulary sets into a creative-thinking and writing challenge. Work with a set of linked vocabulary items, for example things found in the bathroom (*shaver, toothpaste, towel, shower, toilet paper*, etc.). Tell students to imagine that they are alone in a house, locked inside the bathroom. Their challenge is to imagine how they might use the items on the list in a resourceful way to send a message to someone outside, or to attract attention in some other creative way. Let students confer in groups before writing down their suggestions. They do not have to use all the items on the list.

An example using the items mentioned above:

Write HELP in big letters on a towel with the toothpaste. Wait for it to dry. Hang it from the window. Wait for someone to arrive.

7. Setting problem–resolution stories

Try collaborative writing activities, in which individual students each make their own contribution to a jointly-created piece of group writing. Get students into groups of three and give each student a blank piece of paper. Ask each student to write the opening paragraph of a story. The first paragraph sets the scene. Students then rotate papers and read their classmate's opening paragraph. Each student then continues the story begun by the previous writer with a second paragraph, which introduces a problem or complication. Students then rotate papers again and repeat as before. The third and final paragraphs deal with how the problem is resolved.

8. Left hand, right hand

Write a sentence on the board and get students to copy it down twice, holding the pen in a different hand each time. Then ask them to compare the two versions of their handwriting. Get them to describe each set of handwriting (left-handed and right-handed). Ask them to choose adjectives to describe the qualities of their left hand and right hand as if they were two people. Finally, ask the students to imagine a conversation between their own left and right hand. Students write the dialogue down, switching the pen between left and right hands as they switch characters in the dialogue.

9. Hidden song lyrics

Give students a standard writing task, but add a creative 'song lyrics challenge'. As students plan their writing, they also choose a well-known song and find the lyrics. They then select four lines from the song to use in their writing. Their challenge is to smuggle the lyrics into the text as inconspicuously as possible. The others in the class get the chance to read the finished piece of writing and try to identify the hidden song lyrics. This technique can help students get inspiration for short creative-writing tasks. In mixed-level groups, offer this idea as a fun optional challenge for students when doing practice tasks for written exams, such as writing a letter of complaint or reserving a room at a hotel.

10. Write the first sentence

Show students the front cover of a book that they are unlikely to have read, and tell them they will have to write the first sentence of the book. Invite them to ask questions about the book in order to get more information about it. Show them the blurb on the back cover and invite any further questions. Give students plenty of time to write their opening sentences on slips of paper. Collect all the slips of paper and read them out, together with the actual first sentence. Students have to listen and try to identify the actual first sentence

"I like creative story-telling. I start telling a story, and stop where the text lends itself to prediction, guessing, or description. I give students prompts such as what do you think the letter contained? (if there is one in the story), how do you think the story ended?, or create a different ending to the story. Students find these tasks motivating, especially if they can also come up with an illustration."

Ms Andrea Sulyok, teacher of English, head of school, Secondary Practice School of Pécs University, Hungary

10 ways to get teens thinking critically

Critical-thinking activities with teenage students often have memorable and rewarding results. The cognitive capacity of the teenage brain is sophisticated and constantly growing. Teenagers certainly have the capacity to think critically, but they have not always had much practice at it. Activities in the English lesson offer an ideal opportunity to combine language practice with development of crucial critical-thinking skills.

Teenagers sometimes have strong beliefs or a tendency to make snap judgements. This can make critical-thinking tasks especially challenging, as the strength of teenagers' convictions and their tendency to accept things at face value can sometimes interfere with their ability to process complex information in an objective way.

1. Do a webquest about Dog Island

In a lesson on the topic of animals, tell your students about Dog Island – an island uninhabited by humans but home to thousands of dogs that have been sent there by their owners to enjoy a life of freedom. Show them the (extremely professional-looking) website at www.thedogisland.com. The website contains articles, photos and detailed information about how the island works. Prepare a webquest worksheet with questions about Dog Island, which students can answer by searching the homepage. There is, of course, no such place as Dog Island, but most students accept the information at face value, even though it at first appears odd. This is a highly effective and memorable awareness-raising activity, which can help teenagers begin to understand how easily people can suspend their better judgement when dubious information is presented to them in a seemingly authoritative context.

For other hoax websites that can be used in the classroom, see https://teachbytes.com/2012/11/01/test-website-evaluation-with-10-hilarious-hoax-sites.

As a follow-up activity, challenge students to see if they can tell the difference between fake news stories and authentic new stories by playing the Factitious game available online at factitious.augamestudio.com.

2. Compare sports headlines for bias

After a big sporting event, for example a tennis final or football match, find two online reports that contain clear and contrasting bias in favour of one of the two competitors or sides. Divide the class into small groups and give each group the two headlines to compare. Ask them to identify which report favours which competitor, and why. Then give them a short extract from the two reports, and ask them to match the report to the headline. Finally, ask students to come up with a new, neutral headline and report.

3. Become aware of our own national bias

As a follow-up task to the activity above, look at a report in L1 of a sporting encounter between a team or competitor from the students' own country and opposition from another (English-speaking) country. Invite students to discuss whether the report from their own country is impartial, and ask them to find examples of language use that support their claims. Then ask them to imagine how the same events were reported in the foreign media. Finally, show them a foreign-media report in English and ask them to identify differences in perspective. Ask students: *Who is right?*

4. Investigate the power of priming

Find a work of art online that students are unlikely to be familiar with and print it out. A good example is *Portrait of a Man with a Blue Chaperon*, by Jan van Eyck. Prepare three sets of photocopies of the painting, each with a different title, for example: version 1: original title; version 2: *The Jeweller*; version 3: *Beggar in Blue*. Put the students in small groups. Give each group one of the three versions. Ask students to describe the man in the portrait. Then create new mixed groups and ask the students to compare their descriptions. Afterwards, discuss the reasons for any differences in interpretation.

5. Examine the 'halo effect'

Ask students to assess the suitability of a candidate for a job. Provide brief information about the job that is being advertised, and elicit the kinds of personal qualities that an ideal candidate should have, as well as qualities that might create difficulties. Get the students into pairs or small groups and provide each pair or group with very brief information about one of two candidates. Give half of the pairs or groups Candidate X's profile to look at, and give the other half Candidate Y's profile. Ask them to rate their candidate's suitability for the job on a scale of 1 to 10.

Example:

Candidate X: honest, hard-working, independent, often sick, argumentative

Candidate Y: argumentative, often sick, independent, hard-working, honest

When you compare the results, there is a good chance that Candidate X will be rated slightly higher than Candidate Y, even though the five qualities listed are the same in each case. The 'halo effect' means that the first item on a list tends to influence how subsequent items are interpreted. Discuss the outcome of the activity with your students, and ask them to think of other examples of the 'halo effect' in action.

6. Try a version of the *flame challenge*

The 'flame challenge' is a contest in which scientists compete to give the best answer to a scientific question, and are judged by 11-year-olds (https://www.aldacenter.org/outreach/flame-challenge).

Get students to demonstrate that they can understand something complex by explaining it in simple terms. Choose a text on a challenging or complex topic and ask students to summarise and paraphrase the underlying ideas in a clear, simple and accurate way. Ask students to prepare their presentation in pairs or small groups. Invite a number of students to be the judges.

7. Decide what the headline should be

Ask teenage students to imagine that they are editors of the school's student newspaper, and that their task is to write eye-catching headlines for the main news stories. Show them a story about their school; for example:

Teachers and students at Radcliffe Secondary School will be taking part in the Stay Safe Online Day planned for next Friday, 17 March, as part of Newton City Council's Internet Safety Awareness Day. Workshops and presentations led by internet-safety experts will take place in the school's award-winning auditorium, starting with a talk at 9 am by local

TV presenter Lesley North. Radcliffe Secondary headteacher Simon Day said, 'This is an important topic for both teachers and students, so I would be delighted if everyone was able to attend the whole-day event. I am grateful to the school staff for agreeing to rearrange their daily schedules, and am sure that the exams originally planned for 17 March can be rescheduled later in the month.'

Ask students to compete to come up with the best headline for this story. Compare their answers. In order to write a good headline, they will have to synthesise the information contained in the text, and extract what is relevant for their readers. In this case, an appropriate headline might be *No exams on Friday!*

See page 145 of the Appendix for a photocopiable version of this exercise.

8. Use debates to challenge students to think in new ways

Ask students to debate a statement on a topic relevant to their lives. Provide a statement, for example *Homework should be banned in secondary schools.* Ask students to decide whether they agree or disagree with the statement. Divide the room into two sections, *for* and *against*. If there are any undecided students, ask them to join the side they are most comfortable with for the purposes of the activity. Then ask students to prepare arguments for the *other side* in the debate – the side that they do not agree with – and to carry out the debate in this way

9. Approach moral dilemmas from multiple perspectives

Describe a hypothetical situation to your students, for example *A laptop is stolen from an unlocked car.* Put students in pairs or small groups. Ask them to tell the full story from two perspectives, adding additional details in each case. In the first scenario, the theft must be seen as *morally unjustifiable*; in the second scenario, however, the theft must be made to seem *morally justifiable*. This is not a debate task; instead, all students are being asked to try to interpret the scenario in two separate, opposing ways. When they are ready, the students present their stories to the rest of the group.

10. Get them to step into a stranger's shoes

Ask teenage students to think of an example from their own lives when they saw a stranger behaving in a way that they couldn't understand. Examples might be an angry passenger on the bus, or someone crying in a park. Get the students to recall the incident in as much detail as possible. Now ask the students to write a journal entry for that day from the perspective of the stranger whose behaviour they didn't understand. As an added twist, the author of the journal should also describe the bizarre behaviour of the teenager who was watching them. This kind of activity helps students to see things from other people's perspectives, and also makes it possible for them to see that subjective impressions can be misleading.

10 tips for evaluation and giving teenagers feedback on skills

Evaluation and assessment are integral parts of many classroom approaches, and in most cases teenage students expect to be tested and assessed, both formally and informally. Being evaluated is a nerve-racking experience for teenagers though, so we should strive to remain sympathetic to their anxieties. Many of the tips below are therefore designed to make the evaluation process as fair and as student-friendly as possible.

Giving teenage students spoken and written feedback on their work also requires a fair amount of tact and awareness. The key questions to ask about giving feedback are *What kind of feedback should I give? How much feedback should I give?* and *How should I give feedback?*

Unit 32

1. Make feedback manageable

Don't try to correct everything in a piece of writing or speech. It only demoralises students. Besides, students cannot be expected to focus on multiple areas at once. Try to prioritise by selecting one or two areas to draw to a student's attention. It is OK to leave some mistakes uncorrected. There will be other occasions to deal with these.

2. Balance negatives with positives

Error correction is only one aspect of evaluation – pay attention to what students are doing well when they work with language, too. Draw attention to examples of effective language use, as well as evidence of learning skills in action or constructive attitudes towards learning.

3. Notice learning strategies in use

Highlight occasions when students use learning strategies successfully. If a student successfully uses an introductory set phrase when speaking, say, *Nice fluency strategy, there! Did everyone notice it?* Or if a student remembers to illustrate an opinion in an essay with an example, point out the effectiveness of this strategy in your comments. When learning strategies are real and in actual use, teenagers notice them and remember them. If strategies are just theoretical pieces of advice, they are less likely to be remembered.

4. Allow students to see evidence of their progress

Try repeating the start-of-year placement test at the end of the year, and let students see their improvement for themselves. Helping students to see the evidence of their progress helps them to sustain their motivation and reminds all students of the importance of individual improvement as a benchmark for achievement.

5. Prioritise areas for students to focus on

Ahead of a test or assessed activity, let students know the areas of language that you want them to pay special attention to. This can help to prime students to use the language more carefully, and often results in more accurate language use in assessment situations.

6. Let students have a second chance

Teenagers learn at their own pace and in their own ways. Some learn better before a test; others, on the other hand, only seem to learn from their mistakes. Don't treat this as a negative thing. Let teenagers have a second attempt at a test that didn't go well the first time, especially if they have been provided with a chance to do in-between learning.

7. Handle test results sensitively

A poor test result can be discouraging for students. Don't make it worse for them by embarrassing them as well. Don't call out the test scores as you hand test papers back to students. Let them decide who they want to share their score with. If a student is visibly discouraged after a test, provide encouragement, but remain honest. Students know when there is work to be done, so don't pretend that everything is OK if it's not. Focus instead on helping students to identify areas for improvement and to find learning strategies that work for them.

8. Don't leave tests uncorrected for weeks

Teenagers find it particularly frustrating when their teachers impose tight preparation deadlines for tests and assessment, but then are in no rush themselves to do the marking afterwards. Getting tests back to students quickly means that you can focus on strengths and things to work on while the topic is still fresh in students' minds.

9. Don't interrupt or correct students practising fluency

When evaluating speaking, we can only judge students' fluency if we let them speak. Don't interrupt or correct students while they are speaking, but do provide them with help if they seem to be searching for ideas rather than language. Afterwards, highlight one area/strategy to work on, and one area/strategy that was effective. Then ask the student to repeat the task.

10. Allow students to self-correct when practising accuracy

When evaluating accuracy in speaking, give students time to prepare and to collect their thoughts beforehand. When a problem occurs, indicate that there is something wrong (for example, with the same gesture or facial expression that you use to indicate mistakes and slips in class) but do not interrupt or say anything. Give students a chance to self-correct.

10 language games that teenagers enjoy

Games that focus on language, or that provide opportunities for controlled practice can be very effective and popular activities with teenage learners. Try a variety of language games to see which ones your students enjoy the most. Preferences can change depending on the age of your students, with younger teenagers tending to prefer livelier games than older teenagers. There is no absolute need to get students up and moving around the room, though: for teenagers, that's no longer fun in itself. As a general rule, what teenagers are looking for in a language game is an enjoyable activity that gives them a mental break from study. The game might perhaps involve physical movement, but it does not have to.

The games below include tried-and-tested classroom favourites, games based on quiz shows, and other playful twists on information-gap tasks.

1. Grammar auction

This is a well-known activity that can be played in various ways. Collect examples of grammatically correct and grammatically incorrect sentences produced by students in their written work. Put them together in a jumbled order to create a list. Get students into pairs or small groups and give each group the sentences to look at. Students read the sentences and decide which ones are grammatically correct. Each group has the same amount of virtual money to spend. Hold an auction in which groups can bid for each sentence in turn. Each sentence is sold to the highest bidders, who receive a slip of paper with the sentence written on it. The students aim to buy as many grammatically correct sentences as they can. Do not reveal whether the sentences are correct or incorrect until the end of the auction. Then review the sentences one by one, correcting the incorrect sentences along the way. The winning team is the one who managed to buy the most correct sentences. If there's a tie, the team with the most money left is the winner.

2. Extreme cloze contest

This is a very popular activity, but it requires a bit of preparation. Find a short text of about 80–100 words on an appropriate topic and at the right language level for the class. For best results, choose a topic that students are familiar with and already know something about. Make a master version of the text for yourself, with each word numbered. Then create an alphabetical index of all the words contained in the text, showing you at a glance how many times each word appears in the text and in which numbered gap it belongs (see page 146 of the Appendix for an example). For the students, prepare a worksheet containing the title of the text, but nothing else except numbered blanks in place of the words. You are now ready to begin. Get students into small groups or teams and give them their worksheets. Their task is to build the text word by word by guessing the missing words. They take it in turns to guess. Award one point for each occurrence of each word in the text, and reveal exactly where it appears. All students write the words into the appropriate places on their numbered worksheets. Continue until the text is complete.

3. Points drop

Turn a set of multiple-choice grammar questions into a whole-class game. Award the class 100 points at the start of the game. Draw a large four-squared grid on board and label the squares from A to D. Show students the first question and the four ABCD options. Get a student volunteer to record the class's selection on the board, after discussion. They can spread their points over a maximum of three squares (for example, 60 points on A, 20 points on C and 20 points on D*.) Students put most points on the answer they feel is most likely to be correct, but if they are not 100% sure of the answer they can spread their points around. One square must be left blank. In this game, points are lost rather than won. The aim is to lose as few points as possible. Reveal the correct answer by circling it. Mark the incorrect answers with a cross. The class gets to keep all the points they played on the correct answer – in this case, 60**. All other points are lost. Continue to the next question. The students' challenge is to stay in the game until the last question. If they lose all the points, the game is lost.

*

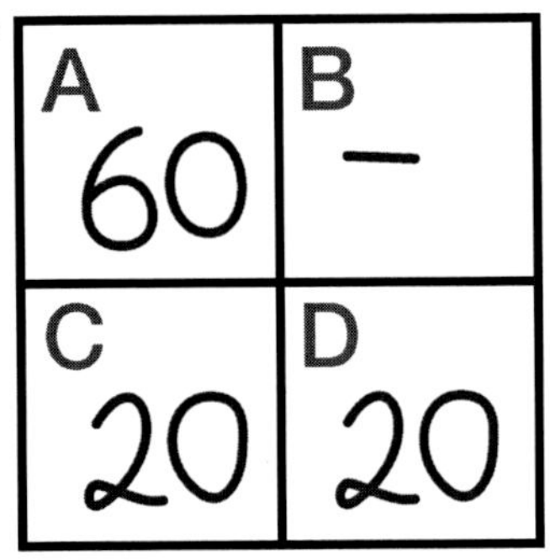

**

4. Transparent multiple-choice

Add a twist to multiple-choice quizzes by asking students to make their answers visible to everyone. Establish hand signals to indicate selections, e.g. *hand up = A, hand on head = B, hand on shoulder = C, arms folded = D*. Show the question and give students some time to think. Then start a five second countdown: students show their answer as you count down from five. They will have enough time to see the answers given by others during the countdown, and so have the option of quickly changing their minds. Students can bluff by deliberately showing an answer they do not think is correct during the first part of the countdown. Students are not allowed to change their answer again once the countdown reaches zero. The more you play this game, the more nuanced students become in using mind-games and bluffing tactics to throw each other off the scent.

5. Penalty shoot-out

This game is based on the format of penalty shoot-outs used to decide the winner in drawn soccer matches. Divide the class into two teams and draw the following scorecard on the board:

	1	2	3	4	5
A	●	●	▲		
B	▲	●	●		

In this example the score is 2-2 after three out of five rounds

Teams take turns to nominate one player from their team to step forward. That player has to answer a revision question. If the answer is correct, it is a goal (shown above as a circle). If the answer is incorrect, it is a miss (shown above as a triangle). Mark the scorecard after each attempt. Whichever team has the most goals after five rounds is the winner. If the scores are tied, play additional 'sudden-death' rounds until one team scores and the other misses.

6. Blockbusters

This game is based on the former quiz show of the same name. It is an ideal way to revise irregular verb forms. Draw the honeycomb-grid playing area (see page 149 of the Appendix) on the board and put a starting letter in each hexagon. Each starting letter indicates the first letter of the correct answer, for example, 'What B is the past participle of *buy*?' In the standard version of the game, each question has a single-word answer. Whoever answers the question correctly can choose the next hexagon to be played for. Students play in two teams, one playing horizontally, and the other vertically. The aim is to win hexagons and to use them to make a connection all the way across the board in your team's direction (horizontal or vertical). In order to win a hexagon, you have to be the first one to shout out the correct answer to a question.

7. Expanding sentences

Write a short sentence on the board. Divide the class into two teams. Teams take turns to expand the sentence by adding one or two more words, making sure it remains grammatically correct. Allow the teams to confer among themselves and to nominate someone from the team to rewrite the sentence on the board, adding the new word or words. The game continues until one team makes a grammatically incorrect move, or is unable to expand the sentence any further.

8. Typing duels

Hold a contest to see which student can type grammatically correct sentences the fastest. You might do this with a group of fast finishers, for example, on laptops, tablets, or even on mobile phones. Choose two competitors. Read out or say the sentence they have to type. The two students compete to be the fastest to type it out without making any mistakes. Allow other students to challenge the winner, or even hold a knockout competition. Use a website such as todaysmeet.com to host the competition: it enables students to type simultaneously in the same virtual room. Whatever is typed will appear in the order in which it is submitted.

9. Alibi

Select two students to play the part of people suspected of committing a crime together. Tell the rest of the class what the crime was, and then inform the two suspects that they are going to be questioned individually by a group of detectives (the rest of the class) about where they were and what they were doing at a certain time the previous day. The only way the suspects can prove their innocence is if their stories match. Give the suspects five minutes or so to agree on their alibi or story. They can leave the room to do this. Then ask them to come in to be questioned, one at a time. The detectives take turns to ask questions and look for inconsistencies in the two stories that prove that the suspects are lying, and therefore guilty of the crime.

This is a classic game, and although it has been around for ages, teenagers often request it. The structure of the game also makes it ideal for practising both simple and continuous past tense forms.

10. Is it true or false?

Turn grammar practice activities based on personal information into a game. Give students a sentence prompt, for example, *watch TV / last night*. Ask students to personalise it by writing a grammatically correct sentence about themselves – but tell them it does not have to be the truth. Students get two points for writing a grammatically correct sentence, for example, *I watched TV last night* or *I didn't watch TV last night*. Students get into pairs. They each try to guess which of their partner's sentences are true and which are false. If they wish, they can ask questions to probe their partner's story. Each student gets a further point if their partner guesses wrongly.

Developing language awareness (grammar, vocabulary, pronunciation)

The units in this section focus on teaching grammar, vocabulary and pronunciation to teenage students, aiming not only to help them value the process of gaining language awareness, but also to give them the confidence and skills they need to learn effectively, both inside and outside the classroom.

The activities assume that, for the most part, teenage students will not be overly enthusiastic at the prospect of focusing on language, perhaps because they associate it with dry and tedious practice activities. A key feature of teaching grammar, vocabulary and pronunciation involves raising students' awareness of the value of language awareness itself. This can be done through discussion and reflection; students will often only find the desire to engage with the language once they have recognised that there is a point to it.

Provided our classroom activities contain a spark of interest or a motivating task, students are generally prepared to engage. If we are able to design activities in such a way that they get students thinking about how they can improve further, rather than merely thinking about what they are getting wrong, then a bedrock of confidence can also be established, giving students the motivation to take part actively in language-development activities.

Many of the tips and activities encourage teenagers to become aware of how they use language already, and to get into the habit of noticing features of grammar, vocabulary and pronunciation in the language around them. Effective habit formation is a fundamental aspect of autonomous learning, and so students are guided to develop habits that work for them, for example, with regard to techniques for storing vocabulary, or for helping them to pay attention to individual sounds. The ultimate aim of the section is to suggest tips and activities that can motivate students to value language awareness by helping them become aware of its essential usefulness. It's only when teenagers stop feeling that language-awareness activities are a waste of time that they can begin to reap the benefits.

10 grammar activities that teenagers won't hate

Grammar activities are generally not crowd-pleasers with teenage students unless important exams are imminent. To discover the reasons for this, it's worth looking at how we present grammar activities to students in class. Teenagers often find traditional use-of-language activities difficult, boring, and lacking in any real-world spark. It's worth remembering that students respond well to tasks and activities that present them with a puzzle, a challenge or an opportunity to come up with an imaginative solution. In other words, grammar itself does not have to be boring, as long as we can find an interesting angle with which to present it to students.

We can also be transparent about what we are doing. There is no need to smuggle grammar into a lesson by pretending that it's something else. The key consideration when planning grammar activities for teenagers, though, is to think about the tasks from the students' point of view, and to try to include an element of personal challenge in order to make the focus on language more engaging and worthwhile.

1. Definitions challenge

Have a competition to see how many words students can define in 60 seconds. Use words and vocabulary items that the students are already familiar with. Prepare plenty of word cards to use in the game, or use any vocabulary revision cards you might already have made. Pre-teach phrases for defining nouns (*It's something that … / It's someone who … / It's a place where …*), verbs (*It's when you …*), and adjectives (*It's used to describe something that …*). Put students into two teams. Before each round, nominate from one of the teams one student to be the timekeeper, two students to be grammar checkers and two students to be definition checkers. Volunteers from the other team take turns to define words from the set of cards. Their teammates guess what the word is by shouting out their guesses. When 60 seconds are up, allow the checkers to decide if the definitions were correct (lexically and grammatically). Award one point for each correct definition. The teams then swap over so that the team members who have just played take on the roles of timekeepers and checkers. Provide help as needed and keep a running total of correctly defined words. The winning team is the one with the most points. As an alternative, get students to invent definitions of non-existent (made-up) words, for example, ***blashter.***

2. Creative gap-fills

Write a sentence on the board containing one gap, for example, *The afternoon in the airport was the ___________ part of the holiday*. Put students into two teams, A and B, and ask the members of team A to think of imaginative and grammatically correct ways of filling the gap (using a superlative form in this case). Each student in team A writes one answer on a scrap of paper, choosing less frequent, less familiar words if they can. Don't let them confer. When every member of team A has chosen a word, get them to count up how many different answers they came up with altogether as a team. Now give team B five attempts to predict the answers written by team A. If team B correctly guesses a word that a student from team A came up with, then team A have to cross that word off their list. After the fifth guess, review the words left on team A's list. Ask them to read out their remaining answers with a short explanation of each to demonstrate that they understand the correct meaning of the word. For example, if their superlative adjective was *most entertaining*, they might give the explanation ... *because we met a guy who showed us amazing card tricks*. If the explanation is acceptable, it counts as one point. Make a note of team A's final score.

Then write a new sentence on the board, for example, *There were six kittens altogether, but we chose this one because she was the* ___________. This time the teams swap roles: each member of team B chooses a superlative form to fill the gap; then the members of team A have five attempts to predict words from team B's list. Compare scores at the end. The winning team is the one with the highest score.

3. Mini-interviews from workbook questions

Breathe unexpected life into grammar-practice activities in the workbook by asking students follow-up questions as you check the answers. For example, if the item in the book is *My father drives more slowly* ___________ *my mother*, first ask one student to give the correct answer (in this case *than*). Before moving on to the next question, respond to the content of the answer in a slightly playful way. Say *How interesting. Would you say that your father is a slow driver, or is it just that your mum drives fast?* Teenagers are not expecting to have to 'own' the content of the workbook items in this way, but usually enjoy the (sometimes absurd) challenge of providing creative answers. Encourage other students in the class to ask their own questions, too.

4. Cause-and-effect brainstorming

Present students with an open-ended puzzle and get them to come up with creative solutions. Begin by setting the scene. Present the following scenario to students, or one like it. (You can write it on the board, dictate it, present it as a gap-fill and elicit answers, or do a picture dictation.)

A boy is standing at a bus stop. He's holding a watermelon. The bus comes and the doors open. A girl leans out of the open door and says something to the boy angrily. The boy looks shocked, says sorry to the girl, gives her the watermelon and starts running in the direction the bus came from. The girl sits down in her seat again, holding the watermelon in her lap and shaking her head.

Ask students to work in pairs. Their task is to make sense of this story, using speculative language, such as *might have / may have / could have*. Listen to the students' ideas first, helping them to ensure that the grammar is correct. Then ask follow-up questions about their story. At the end, decide which solution to the puzzle was the most creative.

One possible solution: The girl is the boy's sister. The boy had been asked by his sister to go to the store to buy a watermelon while she was in town. She told him he could take her bicycle and put the watermelon in the basket on the front. On the way out of the store, the boy forgot about the bicycle and – out of habit – walked over to the bus stop. Meanwhile his sister spotted her bicycle outside the store from the bus window. When she saw her brother waiting at the bus stop with the watermelon, she realised what had happened. When the doors opened, she told him to run back to get her bicycle before someone stole it.

5. Everything's OK – a one-word dialogue

Put students into pairs and provide them with the script for a short dialogue in which each speaker only says *OK* each turn.

A: OK

B: OK

A: OK

B: OK

A: OK

B: OK

A: OK

B: OK

A: OK

B: OK

The challenge is to come up with a communicative dialogue in which the only word spoken is *OK*, so students have to use their imagination.

Give each pair time to decide what they think is going on in the dialogue. They can add any punctuation they want (question marks, exclamation marks, etc.) but they cannot add any words to the script. They will have to think about all the communicative functions that can be expressed with the word *OK*: it might be a question, an agreement, a challenge, an expression of sympathy or an exclamation of delight. The pairs practise performing a meaningful dialogue using only the word *OK*.

When they have planned their dialogue, each pair performs it twice. The first time they can only use the words in the script, but can embellish the meaning with gestures, facial expressions and intonation. The other students guess what is happening. Then the pairs prepare to perform their dialogue a second time. They write down an expanded version, replacing all the OKs with complete questions and sentences. At the end of the activity, students vote for the dialogue they thought was the most creative. You can then focus on any grammar points that emerged from the dialogues. Teenagers are noticeably more willing to focus on language when they have created it themselves.

6. Create flowcharts to support rules of language usage

Get students to interpret grammar rules by turning them into flowcharts. Many coursebooks highlight the rules of language usage in special 'grammar boxes', but teenagers rarely pay them much attention. Making a flowchart is an effective way to help students engage with the rules, and also helps them to check their own understanding of them. A further advantage of a completed flowchart is that it can be tested (and sometimes improved) by other students in the group. See page 150 of the Appendix for an example of how a grammar box in a coursebook can be turned into a flowchart.

7. Relative-clause roulette

Give each student a small piece of paper or card, numbered on one side. On the other side of the card, ask each student to write a non-defining relative clause beginning with *who*, for example, ..., *who speaks three foreign languages*, ... Check the clauses for accuracy. Stick the completed cards on the board in the shape of a circle, with the numbers facing out. Students take turns to choose a number from the 'roulette wheel' on the board. They then have to write a full sentence on the board, using the chosen non-defining relative clause *and* the number on the card. So, if the above clause was on card number 12, the full sentence would also need to contain some reference to the number 12. One possible answer might be: *My sister, who speaks three foreign languages, started learning Spanish when she was 12*. The activity can then be repeated with non-defining relative clauses starting with other pronouns (*where, which, whose*).

8. Images from sentences; sentences from images

Write the following sentences on the board, or similar sentences with the same tense contrast:

A. *When she looked up, he was leaving.*

B. *When she looked up, he had left.*

C. *When she looked up, he left.*

In pairs, get students to discuss the meaning of each sentence, and the difference between the three. Instead of translating the sentences into L1, get students to draw a comic strip of each sentence in such a way that it demonstrates that they understand the order in which the two events happened in each sentence.

The students' drawings could look something like this:

Sentence A

Panel 1: They're both sitting at different tables, reading.

Panel 2: She's still sitting and reading, he's now standing up.

Panel 3: She's looking up at him; he's putting his coat on and moving away.

Sentence B

Panel 1: They're both sitting at different tables, reading.

Panel 2: She's still reading; he's halfway out the door.

Panel 3: She looks up; he's gone.

Sentence C

Panel 1: They're both sitting at different tables, reading.

Panel 2: Still seated, they both look up at the same time and catch each other's eye.

Panel 3: He's putting his coat on and moving away; she's watching him.

Alternatively, provide each pair with a unique set of sentences. When they have finished their drawings and had them checked, students swap them with another pair. Now they have to look at the three images and write the correct sentence to accompany each one.

9. Exclusive answer cards

When doing a difficult gap-fill exercise, write the answer to each question on a separate card. Provide each pair with one of the cards containing one of the correct answers, but do not indicate which question it is the answer to. Do the activity as a competition: each pair tries to get the most correct answers. If they wish, students can decide to show their answer card to other pairs in return for seeing what's on theirs, but at the same time they need to consider how many times they should do this and with which pairs. If they suspect that a particular pair has a good chance of winning, they might decide not to show them what's on their own card. This adds an element of strategy to the activity.

10. Text correction with music

Find a song that your students are not familiar with. Choose a song with a strong narrative, which is at a suitable language level for your students. Reformat the song lyrics to resemble a paragraph of text, and then make five to 10 deliberate grammar mistakes in the text. Tell the students that they are going to read a story that contains some language mistakes. Give them a chance to read through the text and to find as many mistakes as they can. Then play the song. Finally, check the answers together.

"I have tried many different grammar activities with teenagers, and it happened many times that one activity works perfectly with one group, but it does not work with the other group, or at least it does not work that well. It is great to have many activities up your sleeve, and not be afraid to try them out; teenagers love variety. Someone will always learn something from those activities, either you or your students, if you know what I mean;)"

Branka Dečković, English Language Teacher, Medical school, Kragujevac, Serbia

10 ways to give teenagers effective feedback on grammar

Feedback on grammar usually has one of two objectives: awareness raising or correction. Teenagers are not generally keen to spend long periods of the lesson analysing the language, so make sure that grammar clarifications are short: the real objective is focused and informed practice.

Provide students with plenty of opportunities to pay attention to language: encourage them to notice the role of grammar in language and to think about form as well as meaning. Do not worry too much about student errors; they are helpful indicators that students are experimenting with language. Consider them as markers of progress, not as impediments to learning.

When it comes to dealing with mistakes or slips, be aware of the choices that you have. Before deciding on a course of action, think about the type of mistake you are dealing with, the type of activity in which the slips occur, and the type of feedback you think the learner will respond to most positively.

1. Distinguish between spoken and written grammar

It is common for teens to use many of the more informal and idiosyncratic features of spoken grammar (and the grammar of online messaging) in their writing – without being aware that there are different norms and expectations for spoken and written grammar. Raise awareness of the difference between the two by using examples. Collect authentic chunks of informal spoken or online-messaging language, for example, *You gonna be there on time?* Ask students to write them according to the norms of written grammar, for example, *Are you going to be there on time?*

2. Focus on practice rather than presentation

The most effective way to engage teenage students with feedback on their use of grammar is to create opportunities for focused practice. As teachers, we enjoy giving explanations, but teenagers quickly get frustrated when the teacher moves to grammar-presentation mode in response to students' grammatical mistakes. That's when we hear comments like *We've already done this* and *[sigh] We know*. Teenagers are more likely to get grammar through guided trial-and-error practice, and not through listening to the teacher's lengthy explanations.

3. Challenge students to work it out themselves

A guided-discovery approach can be an effective way to give teenage students feedback on grammar. Show students examples of language containing new grammar and encourage them to focus on the form. Elicit their ideas and invite them to try to work out the rules for themselves, providing plenty of examples for them to work with. Treat it as a puzzle: as we have seen, teenagers enjoy a challenge. Once the grammar rules have been established, give students opportunities for further practice.

4. **Revise grammar with real examples**

   As teenagers learn new grammar, there is a tendency for old grammar to become rusty. Look for authentic ways to refresh students' language awareness. One way to do this is to pay close attention to the grammatical content of students' spoken and written work, and to collect examples to recycle in future lessons. If there are recurring mistakes or typical slips that several students in the group are making, be sure to select those. Once collected, the sample sentences can be used as the basis of a consciousness-raising language game (see Unit 33).

5. **Acknowledge good grammar**

   Don't forget to draw attention to examples of skilful and correct use of grammar in your students' work: this can be an effective and motivating way to help students pay attention to form. Get into the habit of commenting on correct use of language instead of simply dealing with inaccuracies. Say things like: *Nice use of the past perfect there!* or *I like the way you remembered to use connectives in that paragraph.*

6. **Keep it short**

   Whatever the feedback given, remember that – with teenagers – *less is more*. The danger of too much feedback is that students can lose their appetite to experiment with the language. Guide and nudge, but keep the focus on using and practising the language. Short explanations provide more time for putting the language to use. A further benefit is that students are unlikely to reach saturation point (or grammar-explanation overload). In some cases, they might even come back to you with questions: a sure sign of engagement.

7. **Think it through**

   Grammar makes more sense when handled with clarity and authority. There is no reason to feel rushed or put on the spot when handling grammar. Sometimes teenagers ask off-topic grammar questions; don't feel compelled to answer straight away. Teenagers will not lose their respect for us if we prefer to plan a clear explanation with good examples rather than give an unprepared and improvised presentation. Say, *That's an interesting question – but it's not easy to explain in two minutes. Let's come back to this next lesson – I can find some materials that will help you to make sense of it.*

8. **Ask for clarification**

   Resist the temptation to jump in with a correction when students make grammatical mistakes in controlled spoken practice. Instead, give students the opportunity to correct themselves. One effective way of doing this is to make a clarification request, for example, by repeating the utterance (to show that you have heard it correctly) and then adding *I'm sorry – I don't understand.* This draws indirect attention to the fact that there is a grammatical inaccuracy, and gives the student an opportunity to correct it.

9. Invite peer correction

Teenagers can sometimes be reluctant – at first – to accept correction from their peers, but with time they often come to appreciate peer correction as a very effective form of consciousness-raising. When a learner makes a mistake, first offer them the chance to self-correct. If they cannot spot the mistake, invite others in the group to step in. Correction offered by a sympathetic peer is often more memorable (and therefore more effective) than that which is supplied by the teacher. Another benefit of peer correction is that it helps to keep teenage learners focused and engaged during grammar-feedback activities.

10. Do not correct all written mistakes

Teenagers are quickly demoralised by the sight of substantial correction, so do not try to focus on all the mistakes and errors in a student's text; instead choose one or two error types and highlight those. This is another effective way to help students notice form, and can provide useful feedback about specific areas that need work. Resist the temptation to rewrite or correct the language yourself; instead, use correction codes, which get students thinking. See page 151 of the Appendix for a list of correction codes.

"Teenagers write longer texts, which could mean a higher margin of error. Still, aim for quality over quantity in feedback. Focus on acknowledging good ideas conveyed; highlight 3-5 recurring grammatical issues critical to the genre and/or curriculum. Be encouraging rather than soul-destroying."

Janice Chan, English teacher at a university in Hong Kong

10 techniques to help teenagers record new vocabulary

Teenagers are creatures of habit when it comes to writing down vocabulary, so our first key aim should be to help them to acquire the instinct of *noticing* useful vocabulary when it occurs in class; we can then help them to discover which method of storing vocabulary works best for them.

In order for teenage students to improve their vocabulary, they need an effective system for storing and recording the new words that they encounter. The tried-and-tested technique of recording new words in a separate exercise book has the advantage of simplicity, but we also need to make sure that – however it gets recorded – the information is going to aid learning.

1. Create a vocabulary section on the board

When new vocabulary crops up in class, always write it in the same section of the board, perhaps boxed off separately. Teenagers sometimes miss the moments when new vocabulary emerges in class; this way they get into the habit of knowing where to look to see if there has been any new vocabulary and can catch up with what they have missed.

2. Start with the vocabulary notebook

Get students to write down new vocabulary in a special notebook: it may not be very exciting, but it's simple to manage and easy to check. Tell teenage students to think of the vocabulary notebook as a starting point for storing new words.

3. Keep apps for after class

Teenagers might want to enter new vocab directly into an app (such as Quizlet or AnkiApp Flashcards) on their phones in class, but there is a good chance that they will then get distracted. Tell them not to use their phones at this stage and point out that a good way to learn vocabulary is to work with it in a variety of ways and to transfer it across a number of formats (for example, from the board to the notebook; from the notebook to an app).

4. Keep an online record of new words

Online flashcard-making programs and apps such as *Quizlet* (quizlet.com) are ideal for storing and revising new vocabulary, and have the added advantage of letting your students create their own group where they can upload the new vocabulary themselves outside class time.

5. Delegate responsibility for uploading new words

Try appointing a vocabulary scribe at the start of each lesson; that student's job is to upload all the new vocabulary from that lesson from his or her notebook onto the group's app or program after class.

6. Get teenagers to 'pre-search' new vocabulary

Rather than always dealing with new vocabulary as it crops up in classroom activities, it occasionally makes sense to get students thinking about new vocabulary as an out-of-class activity in the run-up to a lesson in which those new words will appear. Set students the homework task of researching the meaning of specific vocabulary items from a coursebook text the day before the lesson. In class, go through the words and compare students' ideas. Read the text together and decide on the best definition for the new vocabulary items.

7. Record phrases instead of single words

Whenever possible, get students to record vocabulary as phrases rather than as single words. Phrases offer greater context and are therefore more memorable and easier to grasp.

8. Give students options

Suggest different options for indicating the meaning of new vocabulary (sample sentence, dictionary definition, synonym, etc.), but be aware that in monolingual classes, teenagers often prefer the quickest, most straightforward option: writing down the L1 translation.

9. Check each other's work

Teenage students can often be careless with spelling when copying new words from the board. When students have finished writing down new vocabulary, occasionally get them to check each other's notebooks for spelling mistakes.

10. Share your own techniques

Tell students how you notice and remember new words in a foreign language and share some tips and techniques. For example, if you carry a little notebook where you record interesting new vocabulary, show it to the students and talk about where and when you encountered these words.

"Each week a different student is responsible for uploading all of the new vocabulary from class to Quizlet. It is a really effective way to help students develop a sense of responsibility and autonomy. I've discovered that when students are given this extra responsibility, they always do better in the vocab test, too."

Sándor Jaszenovics, Hungary

10 ways to help teens find the words they need

In order to communicate effectively, students need to be able to express themselves authentically, and this often involves reaching for language that has not yet been taught. Finding the right word can be very difficult when speaking, as there is little or no time to look up new words. Some teenagers prefer to play it safe when speaking. They content themselves with using words they have already learned – even if the meaning of these words does not quite match what they are trying to say. Other students let themselves get hung up on lexical gaps. Such students often stop in their tracks when speaking and have no idea how to continue.

When writing, teenage students can be quick to turn to dictionaries for help, but often without knowing how to use them effectively. Unless students learn how to check that the English translation of the word they have looked up is the correct one in terms of meaning and context, the end results can be confused and confusing.

This unit looks at strategies and techniques that we can use to help students become more skilled at handling lexical gaps when speaking and writing.

1. Don't be a walking dictionary

Resist the temptation to supply students with every word they need. That is not the teacher's job. Provide words occasionally and selectively, depending on how important they are for the context. In most cases, however, we should be looking to equip students with effective coping strategies for handling such situations on their own.

2. Promote flexible thinking

In speaking and writing exams, students will probably not have access to dictionaries or vocabulary resources. When practising exam tasks, encourage students to consider alternative options when they get stuck for a word. If the missing word itself is not vital, get students to use a substitute word instead. Teach students paraphrasing skills for those cases where the missing word really needs to be expressed in some way, for example, *I can't think of the exact word, but it's something that you use to ....*

3. Paraphrase and then repeat

If students get stuck for a word when speaking and look to you for help, give them an encouraging *carry on* signal in order to give them practice at coping with these situations. Afterwards, provide the missing word or phrase, and then ask them to repeat their entire answer again.

4. Get students to make a note

Try not to let activities become punctuated with requests for words. Provide students with sticky notes and get them to write down any words or phrases in their L1 that they think would be useful for the task. At the end of the activity, they write their name on their sticky notes and hand them back to you in preparation for the 'vocab exchange' activity (see tip 5).

5. Create a vocab exchange

Collect students' sticky notes (see activity 4 above) and stick them on the wall next to the board. Then ask students to come up and browse all the notes. When they see something they can help with, get them to write their suggestion directly onto the sticky note. Review the suggestions with the whole class and return the resolved questions to their owners. At the end of the lesson, ask students to return their sticky notes to your desk. Leave the unresolved queries on the wall, and use them for dictionary practice (see tip 8).

6. Recycle newly discovered vocabulary

Using the sticky notes generated in activity 5, begin the class by quizzing students on the vocabulary generated on the sticky notes in the previous lesson. Read out the L1 words and see if students can remember both the English equivalent, and the name of the student who requested it.

7. Work on classroom language

Make a note of some of the more high-frequency procedural utterances that students say in L1 in class – things such as *What's the English for ...? / What do we have to do now? / I couldn't do my homework, because ...*, etc. Wait until you have collected a good selection of these phrases and then write them on the board in English. Go through them to check the meaning, and get students to write them on the last page of their vocabulary books where they will be able to find them easily from then on.

8. Use monolingual dictionaries to check bilingual ones

When students use a bilingual dictionary to find the English meaning of a word or phrase in L1, get them to check that they have selected the right English translation before they include it in the text they are writing. To do this, get them to look up the newly discovered English word in a monolingual learner dictionary and read the definition to make sure it fits their needs.

9. Use a thesaurus

Encourage students to leave their comfort zones when writing. They can do this by replacing tired words and phrases with alternatives taken from a good thesaurus. Remind students to check the meaning of the words they have found by checking them in a monolingual dictionary before inserting them into the text.

10. Ask students to underline words taken from the dictionary

When completing written work, let students use dictionaries if they want to, but make sure that they use them with restraint. One way to do this is to ask students to underline all the words in their writing that they got from a dictionary. This makes it possible to check whether the dictionary is being used effectively or not. Very often, the meaning of the text breaks down at precisely the point where the dictionary has been used, emphasising the need to use vocabulary resources carefully, as well as the benefits of developing effective paraphrasing skills.

10 teen-friendly techniques for revising and recycling vocabulary

For many teens, especially those struggling with English, learning vocabulary represents a manageable challenge. It also gives them a sense that they are making progress with the language. They may not be too enthusiastic about the idea of learning new words, but most teens can at least see the point of it – especially if there is the added motivation of a vocabulary test.

Teenagers tend to be very receptive to vocabulary tests, and giving them regularly increases the likelihood that new words will be learned. However, it's not enough simply to say *go away and learn these new words for the next lesson* – many teenagers do not have the discipline or even the skills to do this effectively.

Classroom activities that help students to revise and recycle vocabulary in creative and meaningful ways work well because teenagers are always on the lookout for something that is both useful and interesting. Such activities can also help students to recall and remember the meaning of new lexis and help them to become better at learning vocabulary on their own.

1. Have a student-led definition quiz in pairs

Give each pair of students a different vocabulary item. Ask them to come up with a definition, using language like *It's something you … / It's a place where … / It's when you …*, etc. When they are ready, have a definitions quiz. Each pair reads out their definition, and the other class members have to identify the vocabulary item from the definition.

2. Play 'Heads Up'

Write the vocabulary items on separate cards. Ask for a volunteer player to sit on a chair at the front, holding the cards face-down in a pack. The player places the first card on their forehead, without looking at it. The rest of the class shout out definitions of the word or use mime and gestures to help the player guess it. As soon as the player has guessed the word correctly, they move on to the next card. The aim is for the player holding the cards to guess as many words as they can in 60 seconds. The player can pass at any time and move on to the next card.

3. Play a team game: Backs to the board

This game is suitable for younger teens. Divide the class into two teams, one for each side of the classroom. Get one volunteer from each team to come up to the board and to stand in front of you, facing their teammates. Write a vocabulary item on the board. Each team races to explain it in English to their teammate. The first of the two players to get it right wins a point for their team. Continue with new volunteers.

4. Categorise words subjectively

This activity works well when teenage students are feeling creative and want to do things a bit differently. Ask students to work with a partner. Refer to the set of vocabulary you are revising and check to see if there are any questions about meaning. Provide two arbitrary categories, for example, *red* and *black*, and ask students to use these as headings. Their job is to then decide subjectively whether they feel each vocabulary item belongs under *red* or *black* – and to explain why. Encourage them to use their imagination. Afterwards, compare choices with other pairs. Teens tend to enjoy the absurdity of this activity, and often come up with highly memorable explanations.

5. Create mnemonics

Mnemonic devices are hooks to help you remember something. Get students to come up with their own mnemonic devices for remembering the spelling or meaning of words and phrases on the list of vocabulary to be learned. Demonstrate with an example: you can remember how to spell the word *believe* with the mnemonic *never believe a lie*. Have a contest to see who can create the most inventive or memorable mnemonic.

6. Tell synonym stories

One of the best ways to revise vocabulary in context is to tell stories. Prepare a brief story (about yourself, if possible) using all the items of vocabulary to be revised. Then replace each vocab item with a suitable synonym. Tell the story to the class and get them to replace each synonym with the original item from the vocabulary list. As a follow-up, students create their own synonym stories.

7. Personalise vocabulary

Ask teenage students to come up with a way of linking each vocabulary item on the list to themselves or their own lives. In some cases this will be straightforward, in other cases it will require a bit of creative thinking. Share examples.

8. Improvise short dialogues with pocket words

Put students into pairs. Give each pair a situation and ask them to make up and rehearse a short dialogue based on that situation. To make it more interesting, give each student in the pair a secret vocabulary item, which they have to work into their side of the dialogue in a believable and appropriate way. As they plan their dialogue, partners look at both words they have been given in order to think of the best way to incorporate them into the conversation as naturally as possible. Students perform their dialogues; the others listen and try to identify the two secret words in each dialogue.

9. Get rid of one item

In the run-up to a vocabulary test, give students the chance to 'get rid' of the vocabulary item they feel is the hardest to learn. First ask them to make an individual choice, and then discuss their choices as a group. When there is group consensus, write the chosen vocabulary item on the board – and then cross it out. Promise students it will ***not*** appear on the test. Teenagers really value this kind of compromise. And don't worry – the discarded vocabulary item will be the one word everyone is sure to remember, even though it does not feature in the test!

10. Make commuting cards

Encourage students to prepare two-sided flashcards on index cards or small pieces of paper for revising vocabulary while they are on the move. These 'commuting cards' are ideal for revising vocabulary out of school, especially in situations when teenagers only have limited time, such as on the bus home after school.

10 ways to discuss pronunciation with teenagers

Although teenagers can usually see the point of learning grammar and vocabulary, they are sometimes resistant to the idea of practising pronunciation. In some cases, this can be attributed to teen self-consciousness, but it is also due to the fact that many teenage students find pronunciation activities difficult. There is a tendency for students to believe that their pronunciation is fixed, or that it is too late for them to get better. The fact that the pronunciation of students is often not assessed adds further to teens' ambivalence about practising it in class.

It is therefore worth spending time in class discussing the topic of pronunciation with teenage students. Until students come to value pronunciation practice activities, there will be little point in doing them, so take the time to discuss the value of practising pronunciation before you make any decisions about the best way to teach it to your students.

1. Compare pronunciation with grammar and vocabulary

Ask students to discuss the importance of learning pronunciation compared to learning grammar and vocabulary. Which is the most and least important of the three? Is there any point in practising pronunciation? What benefits do they see? Conduct the discussion in the students' first language. This will ensure that students are not unnecessarily self-conscious, and will also allow them to express their ideas and opinions freely.

Teenage students sometimes feel that in the age of international English, 'proper' pronunciation is less important than it used to be. It's worth pointing out that although global English indeed accommodates many varieties of spoken English, the topic of pronunciation is still important, in fact arguably more important than ever. With English being spoken in so many different contexts, pronunciation issues can make communication more difficult. Speakers with clear pronunciation are much less likely to be misunderstood.

2. Keep a record of students' opinions

As students do the activity above, listen and make a note of the arguments put forward in favour of practising pronunciation. Translate them into English and display them on a poster on the classroom wall. Refer back to this poster when you feel that students need to be reminded of their own arguments in favour of doing pronunciation practice.

3. Put them in a teacher's shoes

Play students a video or audio clip of a foreigner speaking the students' first language. Ask the students to imagine that they are the teacher of the speaker in the clip. How would they deal with their student's pronunciation? Would they accept it as it was, or would they try to improve it? If so, how? Connect the ideas expressed with your task of teaching them English pronunciation and add any relevant ideas to the poster made in the activity above.

4. Connect pronunciation to speaking and listening

Brainstorming is an effective way of helping students who do not see the point of pronunciation practice to begin to recognise its merits.

In groups, get students to brainstorm ways that practising pronunciation can help both speaking and listening. Compare ideas and display them on the board or on poster paper. Then add your own suggestions to the list. You might mention the following:

1. Speaking: students who have worked hard to acquire pronunciation features such as connected speech, for example, find that not having to concentrate on getting the sounds right while speaking makes it easier for them to retrieve words and phrases from memory. This allows them to extend utterances in a more natural and flowing way.
2. Listening: students who pay attention to pronunciation also find *listening* easier, as they are used to hearing themselves speak, and so have developed a sensitivity to the sounds of fluent English. This means that they are better able to recognise the pronunciation features of the speech they hear.

5. Compare pronunciation to sports and music

Ask students if they play any sports or musical instruments. Get them to describe how they practise, or how their teachers get them to improve. Listen and ask follow-up questions. Then tell students that pronunciation is also a physical activity. Like sporting ability, pronunciation skills can be developed through deliberate practice – especially by working repeatedly on areas of weakness.

Reassure students that pronunciation is not an intellectual activity: they will not have to get their heads around it in the same way as they do with grammar. If students become frustrated about their pronunciation, encourage them not to think about it too much, and certainly not to worry if they can't see overnight results. Remind them that it is like practising a sport or musical instrument, and that deliberate practice is the key.

6. Compare English words across languages

In classes where the students share the same first language, brainstorm words of English origin that are widely used in the local language, for example, *internet, lift, business, centre,* or *supermarket.* Get students to say the words as they are pronounced in the first language, and then as they are pronounced in English, and compare. The word *business*, for example, might be pronounced /biznis/ when speaking in L1 instead of /bɪznəs/, which is what you would expect to hear in English. In international classes, ask students to demonstrate how the words you have brainstormed are pronounced by speakers of their own language when speaking L1, and compare the results.

7. Get students to choose a pronunciation role model

Ask students to find a speaker of English online whose pronunciation they admire. Encourage them to think of this person as their pronunciation role model. Point out that the role model does not have to be a native speaker of the language; in fact, choosing a role model with the same L1 as them arguably makes more sense. Encourage them to find clips of their role model speaking English, and to practise imitating them as well as they can.

8. Explore varieties of English pronunciation

Ask students if they find it easy or difficult to tell where native speakers of English are from based on their English pronunciation. What about non-native speakers of English? Do they have any favourite varieties of English pronunciation? Discussions of this kind help to steer students away from pre-conceived ideas about what 'proper' pronunciation sounds like, and enable you to celebrate diversity. Websites such as elllo (elllo.org) are a good resource for short clips of spoken English delivered by speakers of different nationalities.

9. Tell your own pronunciation anecdotes

An Italian student once complained to me that she couldn't concentrate because she was /ˈæŋgri/. I asked her if she wanted to talk about it. She said no, she wanted to eat something. It turned out she was trying to say that she was hungry – not 'angry', which is what I had heard. We all have our own favourite stories and anecdotes involving real-life situations or classroom interactions where a misunderstanding was caused by pronunciation. Share some of these stories with students and see if they have any of their own.

10. Tell students about the International Phonetic Alphabet (IPA)

Before you start working on pronunciation activities, introduce students to the phonemic chart. Find a poster or ask students to look for phonetic symbols in the coursebook and dictionaries that they use. Discuss the IPA as a potential resource, rather than drilling it. Anxiety is to be avoided. Instead, focus on getting students curious about what the IPA is, and how it might be of use. You could draw students' attention to the use of IPA in dictionary definitions, for example, and point out that the IPA transcription of a word enables them to work out how to pronounce it correctly. This can be of great use when they are studying alone or if there is no one around to help them. See Unit 40 for more details on how to use the IPA in class.

"The 'repeat after me' approach is not effective, because it does not help students to notice what is actually going on with their pronunciation. In class, we talk about how you make the sound, not what it sounds like – that improves awareness, which is the key to good pronunciation."

John Andrade, trainer and teacher, Colombia

10 ways to get teens interested in individual sounds

Awareness raising is the key to getting teenagers interested in individual sounds. Too much drilling can be counter-productive, as students quickly lose interest. Focus instead on finding engaging ways to help students notice individual sounds and how they can be represented phonetically.

Most of the activities in this unit make use of the symbols found in the International Phonetic Alphabet (IPA). The IPA may seem daunting to teenagers who have never encountered it before, so it's important to use it sparingly at first. There are good reasons for working with the IPA: the phonemic symbols show up in many textbooks and dictionaries, and so promote and enable autonomous learning.

1. Put up the IPA chart in the classroom

Display a phonemic chart (showing all the sounds, or 'phonemes', of the English language) on the wall near the front of the classroom. Online and printable versions of the chart can be found at www.macmillanenglish.com/pronunciation/interactive-phonemic-charts. Your teenage students might not yet be aware that there is a phonemic alphabet, in which case they will probably be curious. Use the poster occasionally as a visual aid to focus on individual sounds that crop up in lessons. The idea is not to drill the phonemic alphabet, but to use the poster as a way to get students' attention and to raise their awareness of the English-language sound system itself. Many coursebooks also have a digital component containing an online or CD-ROM version of the phonemic chart; this has the advantage of providing audio recordings of each individual sound.

2. Try guided correction

Writing a single phonemic symbol on the board can give students the guidance they need to correct their own pronunciation. As an example, consider the student who mispronounces the word *cycle*, for example, by saying /ˈsiːk(ə)l/ instead of /ˈsaɪk(ə)l/. Write the word *cycle* on the board, underline the y, and beneath that write /aɪ/. Now the student is in a position to be able to work out what is going wrong – and to put it right. Provide help or ask other students to help if the student does not recognise the symbol /aɪ/. This approach works well with teenagers, as instead of simply correcting them, the teacher sets them a puzzle – and gives them a chance to self-correct. In this particular case, another possibility would be to point to your eye to indicate the /aɪ/ sound. This could be done in addition to – or instead of – writing the phonemic transcription on the board.

3. Tap out words

Use the digital version of the phonemic chart (see tip 1 above) to tap out a word sound by sound, for example, when introducing a new topic. Students will be able to hear each sound as you tap the relevant symbol (for example, /f/… /æ/ … /ʃ/ … /ə/ … /n/). Ask them to watch, listen and identify what it is you are trying to say, in this case: fashion. Students can either write the word down or call it out. For a greater challenge, do the same exercise without audio support. The simplest way to do this is to use the classroom poster and tap on the symbols representing the sounds contained in the word you have chosen.

Unit 40

Unit 40

4. Write messages for the students on the board

Get into the habit of writing messages on the board in phonemic script for students. Students who are not familiar with the IPA will have to decipher the message – but this is actually not as difficult as it sounds, provided that the words themselves are known to the students. An example message that you could write on the board might be: /nəʊ ˈhəʊmwɜːk təˈdeɪ/. Ask students what you have written, and when they have guessed correctly, write the message again in standard English underneath: *no homework today*. This is a good way to get students curious about the sound system of the language, and offers them the chance to notice the connection between the symbols and the sounds they represent.

5. Encourage students to use IPA apps for self-study

Get teenage students to download an IPA app to their phones. The apps by Macmillan (*Sounds*) and the British Council (*Learn English Sounds Right*) are both free to use. Point out that there are three sets of sounds: *consonants* (e.g. /v/, /p/, /dʒ/), *monophthongs* which are pure vowel sounds (e.g. /ʌ/, /iː/, /ɔː/), and *diphthongs*, which are 'gliding' vowel sounds, consisting of two adjacent vowels (e.g. /eɪ/, /aʊ/, /ɔɪ/). Briefly explain what they are and where they are located on the chart. Assign one set to each student, making sure there is an even distribution. In each case, ask students to try to find a word in English that contains the sound, and also a word in the students' first language that contains it, if appropriate (remember that there might be certain sounds that do not feature in any words in the students' first language).

6. Compare sounds in English with the students' first language

As a follow-up to the activity described in tip 5 above, get students into groups of three. Each group should contain one student who looked at consonants, one student who looked at monophthongs, and one student who looked at diphthongs. Produce a copy of the phonemic chart for each group, cut up so that each piece of paper contains one symbol. Ask students to present the symbols to each other by sharing the information they came up with in the previous exercise. All three students should then try to find further examples of words in English that contain this sound and words in L1 that contain this sound. Monitor students as they work, providing help and assistance as required. Compare the different groups' answers. If you wish, you could stick some of the slips of paper onto the classroom IPA poster.

7. Focus on tricky sounds

In groups where the students all share the same L1, collect up all the phonemic symbols that do not feature in the students' first language and write them on the board, together with one or two words in English that feature this sound. Ask students to work individually, dividing the sounds into two groups: sounds I can make, and sounds I need help with. Then do a mingling peer-teaching activity in which students walk around, compare lists, and help each other out whenever they can. In international groups, do the same activity, but select a number of sounds at random instead of focusing on those that do not occur in the L1. This activity works particularly well in teenage groups of different nationalities, where certain sounds that are difficult for some students can be modelled expertly by others.

8. Guess the song from the IPA lyric

If you have an interactive whiteboard, tap out one line from a well-known song using an interactive phonemic chart and see if students can recognise which song it is from. Then ask each student to prepare a similar task, using the app on their phone to practise. When they are ready, invite students to present their lyric to the rest of the group using the interactive chart at the front of the classroom. If you don't have access to an interactive whiteboard, use the poster on the classroom wall. The others have to identify the song.

9. Do a phonetic script gap-fill

Find a short text already covered in the coursebook and use it to create a gap-fill text. Instead of writing words in the gaps, students need to use the IPA. Write the answers on sticky notes and stick them in different places around the classroom. To make it more interesting, create twice as many possible answers as there are gaps in the text. For example, if one of the sentences in the text was I *knew that if I didn't call her she would be angry*, write /ˈæŋgri/ on one sticky note, but include a synonym or alternative answer, such as /ʌpˈset/ on another one. Both answers are acceptable – the students can choose whichever one they prefer. This way, students have more words to identify, and the activity also provides them with an element of choice. Teenagers who do not wish to move around much do not have to – they can try to write the missing answers themselves, or simply get up as often as they want to in order to check the accuracy of their phonemic script.

10. Do a video review

As an out-of-class task, get students to search for short videos online that are designed to help language learners master the pronunciation of specific sounds. Demonstrate how to do this in class, either by exploring a playlist of videos on YouTube, such as the BBC Learning English *Improve Your Pronunciation* videos or by using a specific search term such as *how to make the 'w' sound in English*. The students' task is to watch two similar videos and find three things they liked or did not like about each one.

"My students find it hard to make the aspirated /p/ sound in English, so I get them to place their palms in front of their mouths when they practise. If they can feel the air against their palm as they make the sound, they know they're doing it right. An activity like this is fun to do and also improves their pronunciation considerably."

Ms Tooba Ahmed, Lecturer in English, Department of Humanities, COMSATS Institute of Information Technology, Pakistan

10 tips for building confidence with pronunciation

It takes time and practice to develop pronunciation skills, and the journey can be a frustrating one. Many teenage students lack confidence in their pronunciation or are afraid of criticism, so it is important to be both positive in our approach and sensitive to the difficulties that students encounter.

The suggestions below focus on relieving some of the anxiety associated with pronunciation. There are some tips for helping students to establish the kind of positive attitude about their pronunciation that can lead to increased confidence. There are also some suggestions for teachers who want to give pronunciation activities a playful, goal-orientated focus.

1. Establish a supportive classroom environment

Teenagers are often keen to share clips of people with very poor English pronunciation, but those who laugh the hardest are often the most insecure about their own pronunciation. Discourage students from laughing at the pronunciation of others, and – most importantly – do not tolerate any such behaviour towards members of the group. Remember, too, that anxiety about pronunciation in the teenage classroom reveals itself in many ways. Students with poor pronunciation can be reluctant to open their mouths; students with excellent pronunciation sometimes play it down, or revert to 'school English' in order to be accepted by their peers. Whatever the situation, students' root fear is very often the same: being laughed at by others. When trying to improve students' confidence about pronunciation, our first job is to make sure that they feel secure.

2. Don't try to fix things

Students' pronunciation will not get better overnight, so don't demand too much or be too insistent that students get it absolutely right first time. The aim is incremental improvement, and the way to get there is by providing plenty of low-pressure opportunities for deliberate practice, allowing students to take control of their own improvement over time.

3. Encourage students to be authentic

Ask students what they would like to change about their pronunciation. Then ask them which features of their L1 accent they are content to keep. Point out that there is no such thing as ideal pronunciation, and that it is entirely natural for non-native speakers to retain some influence of their first language. Ultimately, the most important thing about pronunciation is that it is clearly comprehensible

4. Get students to record themselves

Give students a sample sentence to practise. Let them write it down, but encourage them to memorise the sentence before saying it. Out of class, ask students to record a voice memo of themselves saying the sentence. They can do this on their phones. Encourage them to try several times until they are satisfied. In class, put students into pairs. They swap recordings. Ask each student to listen to their partner's recording and give constructive feedback on what features they like, and what features they think could be worked on.

5. Do self-evaluation

As a follow-up to the previous activity, get students to listen to their own recording again in the light of the comments from their partner. Do they agree? Is there anything else they have noticed about their own pronunciation as a result of doing the activity? What feature of their pronunciation are they now going to work on?

6. Break the silence

Students sometimes feel under the spotlight when practising pronunciation. One way to create a more natural, less intimidating atmosphere is to provide some background noise. Try playing loud music while students do pronunciation activities, or explore online recordings of café sounds to play in the background. You can find some examples on the Coffitivity website (coffitivity.com).

7. Get students to listen

When working on connected speech, start by getting students to listen carefully. For example, to practise the phonemic chunk /ˈdɪʤə/ (as in *Did you go out last night?*), first model the chunk /ˈdɪʤə/. Ask students what they can hear. Repeat the chunk a few times and get them to say it. Ask them what they think it means. Then say, *Did you go out last night?* and ask them to tell you the meaning of the question in L1. Don't write the question on the board: looking at the written script often gets in the way of good pronunciation. Don't expect students to master it straight away, either. It can take a while for students' pronunciation to shift from the unconnected /dɪd juː/ to something like /ˈdɪʤuː/. With further practice, /ˈdɪʤuː/ can turn into /ˈdɪʤə/.

8. Get students to read L1 texts with English-like pronunciation

Select a simple text in the students' first language, for example a children's story or a joke. Put the students in pairs and get them to read out the text to each other in an exaggerated English accent. This activity not only provides light relief, it often produces extremely impressive – and confidence-boosting results. The next time the students practise sounds in English, there might even be a noticeable improvement.

9. Take phoneme selfies

Get students to take a selfie of their face as they practise making a particular English sound. Get students into pairs or groups and see if they can identify the sound being made. This activity often results in exaggerated mouth positions, which is not as problematic as it might sound. Very often, it is shyness about getting their mouths into the right positions that holds teenagers back when practising pronunciation. This can be an effective way to counter that tendency.

10. Praise effort

Encouragement is important, but be mindful of the fact that our aim is to keep students working at their pronunciation, so praise effort rather than outcomes. Above all, avoid comparing the pronunciation of individual students. Comments such as *Good job!*, *Nice work!* and *Keep at it!* reinforce the idea that students are sticking to the task, which is the kind of attitude that we want to support.

Keeping it real: additional lesson topics and activities

The final section of the book is a collection of ideas for stand-alone lessons that can be done on those occasions when either there is no book to work from, or you want to do something a bit different with the students. 'Keeping it real' conveys two ideas: authenticity and simplicity.

First of all, the ideas in the units that follow are designed to be authentically in keeping with the kinds of topics and activities that teenage students are genuinely interested in. Unit 42 tries to get to the bottom of topics that work well with teens – and topics that don't. My own experience of working with teenagers and talking to other teachers of teens suggests that 'red-carpet' topics that focus on the rich and famous are out, and down-to-earth topics that look at the lives of ordinary teens are very much in. The units in this section suggest, among others, ideas for activities on the topics of music, online video, selfies, street art, memes and mobile phones.

Secondly, the activities are designed to be simple and materials-light. When it comes to using mobile phones, for example, there are plenty of offline tasks that don't need an internet connection or special apps. We all know what it's like when we have to cover for a colleague at short notice or teach two groups in one room, and it's essential on those occasions not to be too ambitious.

By focusing on authentic topics and setting straightforward tasks that do not require much preparation (by *keeping it real*), it is often possible to design one-off learning experiences that students value and enjoy.

Teenagers seem to spend a lot of time in school being bored, and English lessons are no exception. The fact that a regular English lesson can be boring is not in itself problematic. The problem for teens is when *every lesson is always exactly the same* – that's when they lose hope. The ideas in this section are intended to be a motivating and occasional pick-me-up for both students and teachers. The aim is not to replace conventional coursebook teaching, but merely to provide a breath of fresh air when things begin to become too predictable. An interesting, unexpected classroom activity once in a while (every few weeks, say) can have a transformative effect on the morale of a teenage group. After such a class, students tend to be more motivated to take part in regular classes taught from the book. The mere knowledge that the teacher occasionally does things a little differently can be enough to keep students awake, engaged, and on our side.

10 DOs and DON'Ts for finding topics that teenagers are interested in

Finding topics that teenagers are interested in is a hit-and-miss endeavour. Although it makes sense to look for topics that are relevant to students' interests and lives, there is still every possibility that our chosen topic area – even if it is traditionally associated with teens – will fail to engage our students.

The best way to find topics that work is actually to pay attention to the students themselves, rather than just choosing topics based on our assumptions about what teens like. At the same time, we should remember to respect the distance between ourselves and our students when we choose topics for class. We need to be careful to ensure that we do not intrude too much on teenagers' private lives.

Despite the challenges mentioned, if we keep the following principles in mind, it should be possible – over time – to get better at finding topics for lessons and activities that our teenage students respond to positively.

1. DO take steps to find out what students are interested in

If students complain about the topics in the coursebook, ask them to suggest alternative topics that they *are* interested in. In addition, keep your eyes and ears open in class when other topics crop up, making a mental note of the ones your students seem to be interested in.

2. DO test the waters

The ideal topic is one that teens are both interested in *and* willing to talk about. Remember that there are some topics that teenagers do not want to discuss with their teacher, even if they have a strong interest in it. A good way to test the waters is to show curiosity about topics mentioned by students. Ask them a casual question or two. Pay attention to how receptive they are to these questions, asking yourself if they appear open or closed to discussing it further with a teacher. Steer clear of the closed topics when planning lessons.

3. DO offer choices

Another way to reduce the chances of a topic falling flat is to offer it as one of several options. Instead of saying *I was thinking about doing a lesson on [Topic A] next week. Would you be interested in that?* say *I've got three possible topic areas for a lesson next week: [Topic A] [Topic B] and [Topic C]. Which one would you say seems the least boring?*

4. DO get feedback on lesson topics

Occasionally, get feedback from students about topics at the end of the lesson. Give them a sticky note or a small piece of paper and ask them to write down anonymously what they thought about the topic and whether they have any suggestions. This is five minutes well spent. Even if the students' feedback does not provide us with much information, the act of reaching out to them – of asking for their opinion – is something that teenagers do notice and value.

5. DO focus on young people rather than pop stars

Teenagers are often less interested in the lives of the rich and famous than their teachers tend to assume. They are also more interested in the lives of ordinary teenagers than many of us realise. Bear this in mind when looking for input language to go with a topic. For example, if the lesson is about fashion, a YouTube video of an ordinary teen talking about her favourite T-shirts tends to be far more interesting for teenage students than a similar clip about a celebrity's wardrobe.

6. DO keep it real and relevant

Glamorous, aspirational topics can actually be a turn-off for many, as they seem too far removed from the reality of their lives. Look for down-to-earth topics that not only have some immediate relevance to students' own lives and experience, but that can be of potential real-life use as well. For example, for the topic of inventions, reading about famous inventors is generally less appealing for teenagers than comparing a selection of simple 'life-hacks' from the internet.

7. DO collect your students' ideas

Save the most interesting comments produced by students in the lesson, or make a note of memorable opinions that they have expressed. Use these ideas as a starting point the next time you teach a lesson on the same topic with a different group of students, telling them that the comments were made by fellow students (but not necessarily revealing their identity). Even if they are not that interested in the topic, teenagers are usually interested in the views of their peers.

8. DON'T get too personal

It always makes sense to personalise topics, but remember that we have no right to expect teenagers to share private or personal information about themselves – unless they want to, of course. Default questions to teenagers should be personal but not prying, allowing them to express an opinion without necessarily divulging personal information. For example, on the topic of presents, avoid direct personal questions such as *What did you get for your birthday?* Instead, try something like *What are you glad you didn't get for your birthday – and why?*

9. DON'T limit yourself to resources in English

Just because something isn't in English doesn't mean it can't be useful in the English classroom. Short texts and clips in the students' first language or in another foreign language can be useful resources in topic-based lessons, providing the basis for interesting discussions – and also stimulating language discovery.

10. DON'T lose your cool

Teenagers can be quite outspoken about topics they are not interested in. If we've spent a long time planning a lesson only for a teen to say something disparaging or rude about our topic, it can be hard not to get annoyed. Don't expect too much, and don't take it personally if you get a negative response. Teens are not always very tactful. Try to remember (if you can) that, in most cases, they genuinely do not mean to cause offence.

10 activities using music

Using music with teenagers would appear to be a safe option, but there is plenty to be aware of when designing tasks for the classroom. It's true that teens spend a lot of time listening to music, and that they usually have strong musical interests. Simply bringing a song to the English lesson and using it as the basis for an activity is no guarantee that the lesson will be well received, however.

Use songs that fit your language-learning criteria. Don't just choose a song you like (or that you think your teenage students will like) and try to work out a way to use it in the classroom. For one thing, doing this can lead to contrived activities and unexpectedly difficult language tasks. Another drawback of this approach is that teens are highly judgemental when it comes to music: there's no such thing as a song that everybody likes. Also, avoid using songs that you are strongly attached to yourself. There is a good chance that your students will turn their noses up when they hear it, which sometimes makes it hard to remain enthusiastic about the activity you have prepared. As a general rule, be cautious with your selections. It makes sense to pick songs that your students are not familiar with, or that you know they will *not* like very much. That way, it's much easier to concentrate on the language and to generate interesting discussions.

1. Guess the rhyme

Find a song that features language and content that fit the topic that you are currently looking at in class. Make sure the lyrics of the song have a strong rhyming pattern. Add five to 10 gaps to the lyrics, choosing words at the end of lines that have corresponding rhyming words in other lines. Leave those corresponding rhyming words in. The number of gaps that you put in depends mainly on the length of the song and the level of the students. (If in doubt, put in a smaller rather than a greater number of gaps.) Give students a copy of the lyrics to look at. Ask them to read through and guess the missing words based on the context and the rhyming words at the ends of other lines. Play the song to confirm their guesses. Then look at the language content of the entire song, and get students to do follow-up language work.

2. Incorrect lyrics

Before class, find a set of English lyrics and read them while you listen to the song. Notice any words that have English homophones (for example, *allowed/aloud* or *bass/base*), or words and phrases that sound similar to other words and phrases in English. Make a new version of the lyrics, adding some of these changes to the text. For example, you might turn *It's all about that bass* into *It's all about that base*, or change *watch all the cars* to *wash all the cars*. Give students a copy of the lyrics to read through. Play the song and ask students to identify and correct the lyrics that have been written down incorrectly. This is an enjoyable way to focus on spelling and semantics (in the case of homophones) and also to practise listening skills (in the case of similar-sounding word and phrases).

3. Jumbled lyrics

Find a set of lyrics at an appropriate language level and on a topic that you have been looking at in class. Prepare a new version of the lyrics with all the lines in the wrong order, apart from the first two lines and the last two lines of the song. Get students into pairs and give them the lyrics worksheet. Before they hear the song, set them the challenge of unscrambling the lines and numbering them in the correct order. They then listen to the song to check their predictions, before looking at the text in more detail.

4. Stay ahead of the music

As a follow-up to the previous activity, write the lyrics of a song out on several pieces of A4 paper – putting each line of the song on a separate piece of paper. Make sure the lyrics are written in large letters so that they can easily be seen from the back of the room. Distribute the papers among the students and ask them to form a line at the front of the classroom, holding their papers. Play a recording of the song and tell the students to rearrange themselves as they listen so that they are standing in the correct order. Press pause at the end of the song line if the order is wrong at that point, to give the students some time to put it right.

This activity requires very little technology and gets students off their feet. For something more sedentary that can be done by students at the computer, try the lyrics-typing games at lyricstraining.com.

5. DIY activity

If they would like to, give students the chance to prepare their own classroom activity, using a song that they have selected themselves. This is an ideal opportunity to give students the kind of additional task for which they can be awarded extra credits or a good grade. Students can choose which kind of activity they would like to prepare: it can be a straightforward gap-fill, or they can try out one of the variations described above (guess the rhyme, incorrect lyrics, or jumbled lyrics).

6. Ringtones quiz

Ask students to use their phones to record the ringtones of five friends or family members. In class, get each student to give a short introduction to everyone on their list. The other students listen, and can ask additional questions. They then predict what kind of ringtone they think each person on the list is likely to have, and why they think so. Then ask the student to play the recording of all five ringtones. Students have to guess which ringtone is from which person's phone.

7. Background music shuffle

As an add-on to the Spread out, speak up activity (see Unit 9.6), which uses background music to get students to speak louder during a paired dialogue, shuffle between five or six songs during the activity. Each time you change the song, students have to repeat their dialogue with a new partner. At the end, as a light-hearted challenge, ask students how many of the songs they can recall. If they have been concentrating on the task (and not the music) this should be more challenging than they expect. To make the task even more engaging, choose songs that are thematically linked, and then ask students to identify the common denominator. Play the songs again at the end of the activity if the students find it hard to remember them all.

8. Stories from song titles

Write four words on the board, for example *love, black, fire* and *little*. Get students into pairs or threes and ask them to brainstorm as many song titles as they can that feature any (or all) of these words. Set a time limit for this. Review students' answers and write them on the board. Then invite students come up with a short sketch or story containing as many of the song titles as they can.

9. Talent show eliminator

Find three online recordings of amateur singers covering well-known songs on YouTube. The worse the performances are, the better. Tell the students that they are the judges on a talent show. One of the three acts has to be eliminated. The judges' job is to decide which of the three performances is the least impressive, and to prepare feedback for all three acts.

10. Follow with the volume down

After an activity using a song and a lyrics sheet, play the song one more time. After a few seconds, turn the volume right down, but ask students to keep the song going in their heads. Let it play silently for a few seconds, then press pause. Ask the students to say what the next word will be when you turn the volume up again and press play.

Doing this very often has a positive side effect: teenagers start to sing when you turn the volume down. There is then no reason to press pause: just continue turning the volume down and up again at intervals. This is a good way to find out if your students have any enthusiasm for singing in class.

> *"My students enjoy trying to translate song lyrics."*
>
> **Magdalena Dygała, teacher and blogger, Poland**

10 ways to use online videos with teenagers

Short videos on YouTube and other video-sharing platforms can be the basis for a variety of interesting language-learning activities. Many teenagers spend hours of their free time watching online videos, and so students are usually receptive to ideas that incorporate video, especially if we use short clips.

Remember to choose a video that fits your language-learning agenda, rather than just showing a video for the sake of it, or because it is funny. It also makes sense to use videos sparingly: a short two-minute video can provide enough input for an entire lesson.

Bookmark videos that you think could be developed into a classroom activity, and think carefully about what you want the students to do before showing the video in class. Students can also be encouraged to develop their own activities based on videos that they have found themselves. Always make sure that the videos chosen are appropriate for class, both in terms of language and content.

1. Unpack body language, gestures and facial expressions

Find a short video featuring several people engaged in a conversation. Use the video to practise speculative language. Play the video with the sound off and ask students the following questions: *Who are the people? What are they talking about?* Let students come up with their answers in pairs. Then display a list of emotions on the board (for example, *excited, depressed, nervous, angry, jealous*, etc.) and ask students to guess which adjective applies to which person in the clip. Discuss their ideas. Then play the clip and allow students to re-assess their predictions. Finally, discuss the content of the clip from a language perspective.

2. Create a voice-over

As an alternative to the activity above, play students the short clip with the sound off and ask them to provide the language. Play the clip several times, pausing where necessary. Put the students into small groups, making sure the number of students in each group is the same as the number of people in the clip. They write down their script. Check all the work for accuracy. Then play the clip again (still with the sound off), getting groups of students to take turns to perform their dubbed version of the conversation. When everyone has finished, vote for which version was the best. Then play the original clip with the sound up. Students try to notice as many similarities and differences between their own version and the original version as they can.

3. Cover the screen

An interesting way to get students describing people is to cover the screen before playing a short video of a dialogue. Play the video the first time and ask students simply to notice the voices and any background noises. Ask them where they think the conversation takes place and who they think the people are. Then ask them to give a full description of the speakers (age, appearance, clothes, etc.) based on the content of the clip and the sound of their voices. Compare students' guesses before revealing the screen and playing the video again. Finally, students decide whose predictions were the most accurate.

4. Discuss videos made by other teenagers

Find two short videos (in L1 or in English) made by different teenage YouTubers from the students' own country. This type of talking-head video is particularly popular among teenage students. Choose videos connected to the topic you want to discuss (for example, clothes, gaming, school life, etc.). Before class, watch the videos and (if they are in L1) translate six or seven sentences from each video into English and write them on separate sticky notes. In class, get the students into pairs and give each student a sticky-note quotation. Ask students to predict the content of the video based on the quotation. Play the videos and ask students to identify the part of the clip that matches their quotation. They can do this by writing down the corresponding phrase in L1 that appears in the video, or, if it is in English, to put their hand up when they hear their quotation. Then ask students which video they think has the most views, and why. Finally, ask them to decide how useful and entertaining each video was, on a scale of 1 to 5.

5. Scramble the sequence

Find a short video with a clear sequence of events, but no dialogue. It could be a commercial, for example. Before class, write a step-by-step summary of what happens in the clip. Keep the sentences simple, and do not go into too much detail. Jumble the summary sentences before making copies. In class, divide the class into two groups, A and B. Ask the students in group A to turn their backs. Play the clip to group B only. Then give a worksheet to each student in group A, and ask them to pair up with a student in group B. In pairs, Student B describes what they saw, while Student A listens and numbers the sentences on the worksheet according to what they think is the correct order. Student A can ask questions. Student B is not allowed to look at the worksheet. Finally, play the clip again so that all the students can see it. Check the answers and discuss the clip.

6. Analyse 'fails'

Search for a selection of innocuous 'fail' videos (very short, amusing videos that show people and animals tripping, losing their balance, knocking things over, etc.). Search YouTube for 'funny fails' or something similar. Pause each video before the incident occurs, and ask the students to describe the setting in detail. Then ask them to describe what the person is attempting to do, and to predict what they think is *going to* happen next. ('Fail' videos are ideal for this 'seeing the future in the present' function of *going to*.) Play the rest of the clip and check predictions. Finally, ask students what advice they would give the people in the video, using *Next time …*

7. Do a circle discussion

With older teenage groups, ask one student to bring in an interesting or thought-provoking short clip, possibly on a controversial topic. Watch the video together and ask students to think of one question that occurs to them as a result of having seen the video. Write all the questions on the board and get students to vote on which question they would like to discuss. After the vote, give each student some time to think and take some notes. Finally, have a circle discussion, allowing each student to express their ideas and opinions. Arrange chairs in a circle. Use a ball to encourage students to wait their turn. The ball is passed from person to person, and students have to wait until they have the ball before they can speak.

8. Share a 'How to ...' video

Find an online video that you once watched to get real-life information. Your chosen video might explain how to make a certain dish, how to fix a household appliance, or how to solve a tech problem. Then find two further video tutorials to use as distractors. Prepare convincing reasons why you might have needed all three videos. In class, play the students all three 'How to ...' video tutorials, and encourage them to ask you questions. The students' task is to decide which video you actually needed.

9. Decide on a dessert

Give students the task of deciding what dessert to serve at an imaginary class party. Put them in groups and allow them to brainstorm their ideas. Find three short online videos demonstrating dessert recipes, and play them to the students. They can only see each video once, so get them to make a note of the ingredients needed for each one. After they have seen all three clips, ask each group to discuss the three recipes, ranking them in order of how tasty they look, how much they're likely to cost and how easy they are to prepare. Ask each group to summarise their opinions briefly. Finally, take a vote to decide on the best dessert for the occasion.

10. Get students to 'sell' their requested videos

Teenagers often arrive in class with a request to show the whole group an amusing or interesting online video. If you wish, find time once a week at the end of the lesson to watch one of the videos and discuss it. Ask students if they have seen any memorable videos online recently. Get each student to say why they think their chosen video is worth watching. Ask questions about the content. Listen to different suggestions from several students and then take a vote. Watch the winning video together and then discuss it.

"I get my students to choose their favourite video material. It's a great way for them to practise vocabulary and share ideas about their interests."

Gábor Tarnai, Hungary

10 ideas for making student videos

Teenagers are generally happy to get their phones out to make videos, and – unlike many adults – are usually not self-conscious or embarrassed about seeing themselves on video. Using mobile phones to make student videos therefore makes a lot of sense.

One of the key advantages of getting students to make videos in the language classroom is that it gives them control. Let students delete and re-shoot their videos if they are not satisfied with the outcome. This approach can prove to be very effective, and students often strive to improve the quality of their finished product through multiple takes. Note that it is traditionally quite hard to motivate students to do their work again in order to make it better. Not so when using videos: teenage students tend naturally to set high standards for themselves when they know they are being filmed.

1. Film vox pop surveys

Ask each student in the class to come up with a survey question in connection with a topic you are covering. If the topic is food, for example, one survey question might be *What do you usually have for breakfast?* Get each student to ask everyone else in the class their survey question, and to film each short response. The collected data can be used as the starting point for a classroom project (see Unit 48).

2. Make a no-comment video

As an out-of-class task, ask each student to make a short (10–20 seconds) video of someone engaged in an everyday activity. For example, it might be a classmate looking at their phone, a family member doing the washing-up, or a street cleaner sweeping up rubbish. (If students are going to film strangers, make sure they ask for permission first.) The video should have no commentary. In class, play one of the videos and ask students to create an internal monologue of what the person in the video is thinking. Give them time to write down their ideas. Play the video again, this time with commentary added by the students.

3. Interview a character from the book

As a revision activity, get students into groups of three and ask them to plan and record a short video interview with one of the people or characters featured in the coursebook. All three students plan the questions and answers; then one student shoots the video, while the other two play the parts of the interviewer and interviewee.

4. Practise roleplays

Get students into groups of three to practise roleplays from the book. Ask one student to be the camera operator and director; the other two students take part in the roleplay. As well as filming, the job of the camera operator is to give feedback and make suggestions for improving the quality of the roleplay. Encourage them to shoot several takes.

5. Film mini-dramas and re-enactments

Bring coursebook texts to life by inviting students to film re-enactments of the events described in texts. This kind of activity is unlikely to appeal to all teenage students, but there are some who will enjoy it. Offer this activity as an optional out-of-class task for students to carry out with their friends in pairs or small groups. The following lesson, play the videos to the rest of the group for comments and feedback.

6. Choose an image to discuss

Present students with a selection of online images to browse out of class. The images might be linked by topic, or they might all be by the same artist or photographer. Tell each student to decide which image that they feel is the most interesting and to think about why. Ask them to plan what they would like to say about the chosen image. Get students working in pairs. Ask them to film each other talking about the image they have chosen. This can be done either in class or between lessons. Get students to upload their videos to your class site, together with the corresponding image. In the following lesson, watch the videos together and discuss them.

7. Introduce a video

Get students to make a video about a video. Before sharing an online video that they would like the whole class to watch (see Unit 44.10), ask students to make a video of themselves talking about the video. Give them some time to prepare, perhaps asking them to make the video outside class, with the help of a friend or classmate.

8. Make a *How to ...* video

As a follow-up to working with online *How to ...* videos (see Unit 44.8), invite students to film and upload their own *How to ...* video. The topic of the video is up to students: it can be something connected to the topic being covered in the syllabus, or students can be free to choose.

9. Make a review video

Ask students to film themselves giving their opinion of something they have recently tried out or seen. It might be a new video game, a new pizza restaurant or a recent football match. Students can film the videos at home, or get a friend to help them. When they are ready, get students to share their video with others in the group via your online group page.

10. Respond to a video

Get students to make a video about another student video. As a follow-up to one of the activities above, ask individual students to film and upload their comments and feed back to their classmates.

10 ideas for using selfies, street art and internet memes

The ideas in this unit focus on making use of the kinds of images that appeal to many teenage students, and that are relevant to their everyday lives. Selfies (photographs taken of yourself on your phone) are probably more commonly associated with teenagers than with any other age group. There are several simple ways to get students taking selfies to illustrate language-learning points – and to use the selfies already on their phones.

Teenagers tend to notice the street art and graffiti around them, and to have strong opinions about it, too. We can use images of this kind as the basis for interpretive activities and debate tasks. Internet memes (stock images with added captions) can also be put to creative use in the classroom, especially because many teenagers are already familiar with memes and are interested in sharing them with their friends.

Activities based on selfies, street art and internet memes can also be given a creative and interactive twist, making them both memorable and motivating. In order to share and distribute the images in the activities below, use an online class group or create a class group on an instant-messaging app.

1. Set theme-word tasks with selfies

Give students a theme word or topic such as *freedom*, and ask them to give a personal interpretation of the theme word in the form of a selfie taken outside class. Encourage them to use their imagination when carrying out the task and to be as creative as they wish. Some may want to explore imagery associated with the word *freedom* in their photo, others might want to show the literal meaning of the word in some way. Collect all the selfies online, and then ask other students in the group to comment on each photo, in each case guessing where the student is, what they are thinking, and what they are feeling. See the 'Homework selfie' idea (Unit 30.4) for another way of using out-of-class selfies.

2. Spot the difference with selfies

Ask students to look through their phones and find a selfie that was taken in school. Then ask them to re-create that selfie as accurately as they can. Finally, get them to compare the two selfies side-by-side and to write down as many differences as they can between the two images.

3. Group-selfie speech bubbles

Highlight the language or structure that you would like the students to practise, for example *making offers and invitations*. Working in threes and fours, ask students to plan a group selfie in which they can act out an offer or invitation. When they are ready, students take the selfie and edit it by adding appropriate text in the form of speech bubbles. Most teenagers do this already when sending selfies to their friends. When they have finished editing, get them to upload the selfie to your online group, where other students can add comments and feedback.

4. Get feedback via selfies

Use annotated selfies as a way of getting short feedback and opinions from students on topics or lesson activities. At the end of class, give students a prompt, such as *How helpful did you find today's lesson?* Ask each student to take a selfie (with an appropriate facial expression, if they like). Then get them to edit the picture by adding a speech bubble or a text overlay. Finally, ask students to upload their images to your class online group.

5. Invent graffiti back stories

Several days before the lesson, ask students to take a photo of some street art or graffiti in the town where they live. In class, get students into pairs or small groups, and ask them to compare pictures. Ask *Who was the artist? What did they draw/write? Why do you think they did it? What do you think happened as a result?* Ask students to invent a back story for every picture. Display the pictures and get students to write or tell their back stories to the rest of the group.

6. Make a graffiti mind-map

As a follow-up to the activity above, write *Graffiti: art or vandalism?* on the board. Let students look at all the images used in activity 5 again. Then ask them to think individually about each image: would they categorise it as an example of *art* or *vandalism*? Then get students to discuss their answers in pairs. While they are doing this, begin two mind-maps. Write *Graffiti = art?* in the middle of a piece of flipchart paper, and draw a circle around the question. Then make another one with the question *Graffiti = vandalism?* Stick the posters on the board. Invite students to explore the questions together by contributing to each mind-map by adding their thoughts and comments.

7. Discuss controversial street art

If your teenage students are ready and able to discuss art in a broader social, political and economic context, try the 'Choose an image to discuss' activity (see Unit 45.6) using the work of the controversial street artist, Banksy. Direct students to a gallery of Banksy's work (for example, banksy.co.uk) and ask them to choose an image to discuss from there.

8. Get students to explain memes

Tell students that you are interested in getting up-to-date knowledge about the latest internet memes (stock images with added captions that go viral on social media). As an optional out-of-class task, students pick one meme each to explain to the teacher. Each volunteer chooses a meme and creates a presentation containing two or three examples of that meme. Each well-known meme has its own theme, so, for example the *Success Kid* meme is used to celebrate the small, sweet, personal victories in life, while the *Unhelpful High School Teacher* meme is used by students worldwide to showcase examples of exasperating teacher behaviour and double standards. Ask students to research the history of their chosen meme (there are dozens of them), including any information about the people who feature in the standard image used. They should aim to explain the usage of the meme as it applies to real-life situations.

9. Hold a meme contest

Ask students to create their own version of a popular internet meme, using a meme generator, such as https://memegenerator.net/. The meme should be relevant to your group, and could refer to the content of what you have been studying, or to recent classroom events. Set this as an out-of-class task. Get students to print their memes and bring them to class. Stick the students' work up around the room to create a meme gallery. Get each student to vote for their favourite piece of work.

10. Story-telling with memes

Create a simple set of slides containing five meme images that are well-known to the students (without any accompanying text). Share the slides with the students and ask them to create a story incorporating all five memes. Give students time to plan their story. When they are ready to present, get them to tell their story as a presentation. They should use the meme slides to punctuate or reflect on the key events of the story as they tell it.

> *"Memes are tiny units of (pop)culture gone viral, most commonly in the form of funny captioned pictures and videos found on social media. Most teens will encounter memes on a daily basis and teachers can use memes to start conversations about various trending topics, highlight cultural stereotypes or grammar points in the pictures as well as teach chunks of language. Or simply use them to connect with your students, perhaps as funny ice-breakers at the beginning of the lesson."*
>
> **Nina Jerončič, teacher of English and German, Slovenia**

10 more ways to use mobile phones

It makes sense to use mobile phones when working with teenagers, but it needs to be done purposefully, selectively, and always with a specific goal in mind. Before using mobile phones in class, ask yourself why you are doing it. Think about your language-learning goals for the lesson and bring in mobile technology whenever it appears to be the most appropriate solution. There are many situations in which using a mobile device *is* the simplest, most appealing and most time-efficient way of achieving our objectives. This is particularly true in the case of last-minute substitutions or situations when you do not have appropriate teaching materials to work from.

Using mobile phones for no particular reason, or simply because teens like using their phones, can lead to their quickly veering off topic and browsing distractedly. In these cases, mobile phones can actually get in the way of learning.

Remember that there is much that can done with the basic functionality of a mobile phone, so explore activities that do not require special apps or internet connectivity. Students do not need to be online; in fact, learning outcomes with mobile phones are often just as satisfying if the devices are offline.

1. Set the language display to English

Ask teenage students to set the language display on their phones to English. Then give them an offline task to perform, such as selecting a new homescreen photograph from their gallery, or setting an alarm to go off for the following morning. Afterwards, ask them if they noticed any new language while carrying out the task. As a follow-up, ask the students to keep the language display on their phones set to English for one week. Get them to keep track of any new language they learn as a result, or to rate the difficulty of handling the phone in English on a scale of 1 to 5.

2. Change the screen display to black and white

This task can be performed either while the phone is still set to L1 or after it has been changed to English. Get the students to change the screen display on their mobile phones to black and white ('greyscale'). If they can't work out how to do it themselves, get them to search online for instructions. Ask them to keep the black-and-white display for 24 hours, and to notice how it affects the way they use their phone. Get them to judge whether they spend more or less time on their phones as a result, and ask them to notice which apps felt better or worse to use in black and white. Next lesson, get the students into groups and ask them to share their impressions. Point out that this technique is sometimes suggested as a way to help people reduce the time they spend on their mobile phones. Ask students for their opinions – both about the issue of phone over-use and the suggested solution.

3. Invent a photo contest

Ask students to browse the photo gallery on their phones and to select a photograph taken during the last week. Get them into pairs and invite them to briefly describe the photo, and to say where they took it and why they selected it. Now explain that each pair must nominate one of the two photographs for an imaginary 'Picture of the Week' contest for your town. (At this point, students might want to go back to find a 'better' photo –

don't let them! The task is about thinking creatively, not about finding the best photo.) Ask the students to prepare a brief presentation in which they explain how their photograph represents an important aspect of life in your town. In order to do this, students will have to be creative and inventive. For example, if the chosen photo shows a group of friends in a café, the students might talk about *cool places in the town where friends can hang out together*. If the chosen photo shows someone sleeping on a bus, they might take a different angle and discuss the *peacefulness and tranquillity of the town*. Listen to all the presentations (or invite several pairs to volunteer) and then get the class to vote on the best one. As a possible follow-up, ask the winners to share their photo to your online group, where all the students can leave a comment.

4. Record a mystery audio clip

Make a five-second audio recording on your phone during your out-of-school time. The clip should contain speech, preferably – but not necessarily – in English. You might record part of a transaction (for example, buying a coffee) or a free-time activity (for example, watching a movie). Play the clip to students in class and get them to guess where you were and what you were doing. As an out-of-class activity, set the students the same task. The next lesson, get them into groups and ask them to play the clips to each other and to answer the same questions. Finally, do a translation task. For clips in L1, ask the students to translate what they heard into English; for clips in English, they do the opposite. Alternatively, ask students to extend the clips, imagining what was said next in each case.

5. Design new icons

Show students a screenshot image of a mobile-phone homescreen showing the icons with the names of the apps blocked out. Ask students to identify the various icons and apps. When you have done that, choose five icons and ask students to describe what each icon depicts, and what it is supposed to represent. Now get students to look at the homescreen on their own phones and to choose three icons that they don't like, or that they don't think represents the concept of the app very well. Invite them to redesign the three icons (digitally or on paper). Finally, get students to show their new designs to the class. In each case, the rest of the group tries to guess what the new designs represent; the designer then explains the thinking behind the new icons.

6. Make a street-view quiz

If students' phones are connected to the internet, ask them to open Google Maps. Get them to select a location of their choice, and then to use the street-view function to look around. When they have found an interesting perspective, get them to take a screenshot and save the image to their phones. Collect the saved images and combine them in a single gallery. Show all the pictures one by one. In each case, students are allowed to ask five questions before guessing the location. The student responsible for each picture should be the one to answer the questions.

7. Use mobile polls

Anonymous polling apps, such as mentimeter (mentimeter.com), are an effective way to gauge the opinion of teenage students. Students use internet-enabled phones to answer polls or survey questions, and the results are instantly collated and displayed on the main classroom monitor. Use the polls for housekeeping questions (such as the best day to schedule a test), or incorporate them into language-learning activities. The anonymity provided can give teens a vital sense of security and empowerment.

8. Create interactive quizzes

Mobile quizzing apps, such as kahoot (kahoot.com), have quickly become a popular option for designing real-time, multiple-choice quizzes for students. In order to take part, students need a mobile device with internet connectivity. Ask students to compete as a pair or small group – this allows them to confer briefly when each question appears. The teacher shares the previously prepared quiz page and tells the students the kahoot access code, which is automatically generated when the quiz is saved. Students then join the quiz room and think of a name for their pair or group. This name will be visible on the main classroom screen. The multiple-choice questions appear on the main screen, and students select their answer on their phones or tablets. Points are won for correct answers, and for speed of response. Results are collated and the running totals are displayed on the main classroom monitor after every question. Teenagers can also design their own quizzes for the rest of the class to tackle in the lesson.

9. Set reminders

Get students to use the alarm-clock function on their mobile phones to set out-of-class reminders. Agree a time when the students will be out of the classroom, and get everyone to set their phones to give them a notification at the agreed time. Later, when they get the alert, students have to perform a designated task. The task can be to take a photograph of their immediate surroundings, to record an audio memo describing what they are doing, or to compare a pre-written prediction of what they think they will be doing with what they are actually doing at the time.

10. Be respectful

Whether or not you use mobile phones in the classroom, each student will probably have a phone in their pocket or in their bag. Establish ground rules for switching phones off or to airplane mode unless otherwise requested. Sometimes (but in the case of teenagers, very rarely) a student's phone will ring unexpectedly during the lesson. Handle any unwelcome phone interruptions assertively but respectfully. Never humiliate students.

10 ideas for projects with teenagers

Project lessons provide a natural way of activating language and putting it to use in meaningful ways. A classroom project can extend and personalise topics covered in class, combining both individual work and work done in small groups to help students consolidate their learning, improve their interpersonal skills and express their own ideas and opinions.

Naturally, project work is best suited to teaching situations where there is a certain amount of flexibility regarding the syllabus: project activities usually involve closing the coursebook, so it is important to be sure that you have enough time at your disposal to fit projects into your schedule without having to cut corners elsewhere as a result.

Ultimately, project work can be extremely motivating for teenage students; it can also help to develop other important learning skills. It allows students to think, research and present their ideas. Furthermore, by promoting independent language activation and collaborative working methods, it can have a positive impact on the learning environment of the classroom.

1. Design a new school timetable

Ask students to think individually about how they would change the school timetable to make it more useful and manageable for them. Encourage them to think about both scheduling (lesson times) and content (subjects on the curriculum). Ask them to justify their ideas, and also to think about what is logistically reasonable. Put students in small groups and let them share ideas. See if they can settle on a compromise that is acceptable to everyone. Finally, ask them to design their new timetable and present it to the rest of the group.

2. Suggest improvements to the school

As a follow-up or alternative to the activity above, ask students to think about ways in which the infrastructure of the school could be improved. Agree on an imaginary sum of money that could be spent, and ask students to think (first individually, then in groups) about possible improvements that could be made to the school building or to classroom equipment. As above, make sure students avoid obviously unrealistic proposals. Follow the same procedure as above.

3. Design a group avatar or profile picture

Get students into groups of three or four. Find a small sample of online avatars or profile pictures, including some abstract and figurative images. There is a good collection at www.avatarsdb.com. Ask students to work together to interpret the avatars or pictures: what do the images reveal about the people who use them? Then give groups the task of designing their own group avatar, incorporating their attitudes about English and their personal interests and concerns. Students should draw their group design; afterwards, if they like, they can use an online tool to create a digital version. Display the finished images and ask students to interpret each other's designs.

4. Create a school survival kit

Ask students to think individually about the biggest challenges they face in the course of a typical school week. Get them into pairs or groups and ask them to listen to each other's concerns. Then ask them to come up with suggestions for a practical survival kit that could help them to get through the week ahead. Encourage them to think practically, but also to use their imagination and creativity. Ask each pair or group to decide on seven objects or items that they would put in their school survival kit. They might be things such as energy bars to eat before boring lessons, headphones to wear before and after class, or GPS locators to find their friends quickly during breaks. Share the finished ideas and get students to vote on which of the proposed kits they think would be most appropriate to supply as standard to new students enrolling in the school.

5. Dig deeper

Use the data collected in survey activities to identify further research questions. For example, as a follow-up to the 'Vox pop surveys' idea (see Unit 45.1), first ask students to display the results of their survey in the form of a bar chart or pie chart. Put students into pairs and ask them to brainstorm further questions that they may have as a result of looking at their data. Then ask them to choose one of these questions, and to conduct a follow-up survey using the new question that they have just identified. They carry out the second survey together, and then collate their results in a new poster or display. Ask each pair to present their findings and conclusions to the rest of the group.

6. Conduct an anonymous public-space survey

At the start of the class, show students Candy Chang's Before I Die … TED talk* and ask them to discuss their reactions in pairs. Then ask students to brainstorm questions and prompts they could ask classmates and passers-by to respond to anonymously (such as *Something that makes me sad is …* or *The best part of my day today was…*). Put students into groups of four or five and ask them to compare the questions they have generated. Then ask them to decide on which prompt or question they would like to use for their survey. Give each group a sheet of poster paper and ask them to write their prompt or question on it. The posters can then be displayed around the classroom or in the school corridors. Attach a pen or pencil next to each poster and indicate that whoever reads it can add their own thoughts. After an agreed time (20 minutes for a classroom poster, or a couple of days for a corridor poster), the groups retrieve the poster they made and reflect on the comments received. Students can then present their results and conclusions to the rest of the group.

* www.ted.com/talks/candy_chang_before_i_die_i_want_to

The six-minute talk describes a community art project in which giant chalkboards are left in public spaces, and passers-by are encouraged to write on it anonymously about their hopes, fears and dreams.

Unit 48

7. Interview an older relative

In order to help students practise using the present and past tenses and the present perfect to talk about how everyday life has changed over time, encourage them to come up with questions they could ask a grandparent, older relative or elderly neighbour about their lives in the past and today. Ask students to conduct short interviews in L1 outside class, and to translate them into English. In class, get students into small groups. Ask them to share their findings and to collect the most interesting responses. Students display their data in the form of a poster. When they have finished, they present their posters to the rest of the class.

8. Imagine and discuss the technology of the future

Introduce the topic by showing students pictures of devices or objects that are now rarely used or obsolete. Examples might be a rotary-dial telephone, a road map or a floppy disk. First ask students to identify the objects or devices and then ask why they are no longer used very much, and whether life is better or not as a result. Then ask students to imagine the role of technology in students' lives 20 years from now. Ask them to imagine ways in which technology will have made their lives easier, and ways in which it will have made their lives worse. They write sentences 'looking back on the present' from the perspective of a student in the imaginary future. Give them a few examples to get them started, such as *When I was a student, we had to learn from heavy books, which we carried to school in a bag* ☹ or *When I was a student, we didn't have to wear tracking devices* ☺. When they have finished, get them to collect their ideas in the form of a poster.

9. Design and pitch a new product

Get students working in small groups. Provide each group with two paper plates, six plastic drinking straws, a plastic cup, some scissors, some sticky tape and coloured pens. Their task is to come up with an idea for a new technological or labour-saving device, and to build an illustrative model out of the materials they have. Working together, they should brainstorm ideas, decide on a product name, build the model and prepare to pitch it to a group of potential investors (played by the teacher and selected students). When all the models and presentations are ready, groups take it in turns to pitch their product and answer questions. (Be aware that although this activity works very well, it requires at least two lessons.)

10. Hold a problem-page clinic

Ask students to think about any difficulties, anxieties or problems that they are having with their English studies. Working individually, get students to write a short letter to a sympathetic stranger (or agony aunt) describing their difficulties. They should put it inside an envelope and write a pseudonym on the front. Collect all the envelopes. Now ask the students to play the role of agony aunt. Distribute a letter to each student, and ask them to write a considered, constructive and sympathetic response, which they should put inside the envelope. Collect all the envelopes and spread them out on a desk at the front of the classroom. Invite students to locate their own envelope and take it back with them to their seat, where they can read the advice they have been given. Finally, ask students to compare the experience of writing about difficulties and responding to others' difficulties. Which was harder? Which felt more beneficial? In what ways was the activity helpful?

10 teen-friendly formats for presentations

Many of the activities contained in other units of this book can be used as the basis for student presentations, as can the extension and activation questions contained in most student coursebooks. The aim of this unit is therefore not to provide topics for presentations, but to suggest presentation formats that are likely to appeal to teenage students.

One thing we need to keep in mind when thinking about presentations is the fact that many students do not enjoy them. Teenagers often find presentation activities dull, while the activity of public speaking itself is highly stressful for many students. The techniques below are intended to make the challenge of giving a presentation engaging for students, while also relieving some of the pressure associated with speaking in front of others.

1. Get the audience to turn their backs

Before a student begins their presentation, occasionally get the other students to turn their backs so that they can hear the speaker, but not see them (think *The Voice*). This reduces the pressure considerably, and also primes the audience to listen carefully, as they will not be able to see any of the visuals contained in the presentation. After the presentation, get the students to turn around and then ask the speaker to repeat the presentation, this time with everyone watching.

2. Set up stalls

In the final stage of a project activity (see Unit 48), one possible presentation technique is to get each group to set up a stall and to allow selected students from each group to walk around the room, listening to short presentations at each stall, just like at a science fair. This technique generates simultaneous presentations that can be repeated several times to new audiences, and also ensures that audience numbers will not be intimidatingly large.

3. Practise 'elevator pitches'

Instead of always asking students to give detailed presentations, occasionally give them the option of condensing their ideas into a short 90-second summary – similar to an 'elevator pitch' situation, in which you only have a few seconds to tell someone your key message.

4. Do your partner's presentation

There is a lot at stake when giving a presentation: students sometimes feel that they are being judged on the basis of many things at once: their language, their ideas and their qualities as a speaker. One way to relieve some of this pressure is to get students into pairs and to ask each student to go through their presentation with their partner. When the time comes to present, each student has to deliver their partner's presentation, not their own. This creates a reduced sense of responsibility for the content of the presentation, which can have a liberating effect on performance.

5. One slide per student

Create a short slide presentation on a revision topic. Make sure that the number of slides is the same as the number of students in the group. First go through the slides and allocate one slide to each student. Give them some time to plan what they might say. Then give the entire presentation yourself, as students listen. This way, students have a chance to compare their own ideas with yours. If they like, they can incorporate some of your ideas and language into their own planned commentary. Finally, do a group presentation, in which the role of speaker passes from student to student with each new slide.

6. Record presentations at home

Allow students to write and record their presentations from home, using a screen-capture and audio/video-capture tool such as Jing (www.techsmith.com/jing-tool.html).

7. Bring in interested listeners

When the topic of presentations is directly connected to students' opinions about school life (for example, activities in Unit 48.1 and Unit 48.2), invite a small number of other students or senior teachers from the school to sit in and to respond to the content of the ideas, rather than to the language used. Organise a separate occasion for this, after the initial project lesson. This time it's the ideas that matter, not the language, so allow the students to present in L1 this time. Next English class, discuss the feedback received from the various stakeholders who were there.

8. Fixed slides, surprise topic

Build a short (and no doubt rather ugly) slide presentation made up of generic clipart and stock images. Make sure there is no text on the slides. Show it to the students without commentary. Then give each pair a different topic. Their task is to create a short presentation about their given topic using the slides you have created. Students are not allowed to delete or add any new slides, and may not change any of the images or the order of the slides. They may, however, add text to the existing slides. Share a copy of the slides with the students so that they can prepare their presentations and add any text they might need. The resulting presentations are always entertaining; teenage students seem to thrive on making the best of a slightly absurd situation

9. Random slideshow: basic

Create a simple slide presentation on a topic area that the students have been studying in class. Create seven or eight slides with appropriate headings and images. Tell students that the next lesson they will have to deliver your presentation using your slides – without having seen any of them in advance. Do not show them the slides or reveal any of the content other than the broad topic or subject of the presentation (for example, 'My daily routine' or 'Healthy eating'). Teenagers respond to this task in different ways: more conscientious students tend to look over the topic at home just to be on the safe side; more adventurous teens, meanwhile, revel in the impromptu aspect of the task and enjoy the challenge of thinking on their feet.

10. Random slideshow: advanced

This is a much more challenging version of the activity described in point 9, recommended for advanced teenage students who love an absurd challenge. Create a selection of truly random presentations. The titles of the presentations should be fairly broad (for example, *21st Century Life*), but make sure the slides have little connection to the topic and that there is no discernible continuity from slide to slide. To make it even more absurd, choose images and headings for each slide that make very little sense (for example, a picture of a rabbit with the heading *Politics is complicated*). Let students tackle the presentation in pairs. First, tell them their title (a different one for each pair) and give them five minutes to think. Do not show them the slides. Then ask them to come to the front and deliver their presentation, making sense of the ridiculous slides in the process. No one expects the presentation to be any good – how could it be? – so the pressure is off. Paradoxically, the results are often extremely memorable. Once students are familiar with the format, invite them to write their own random slideshows for other students to perform.

"When running in-class presentations there can be a few different things to manage so allocate them out to students. For example, you might set time limits on a presentation so one student in the audience could be in charge of timekeeping and signal to a speaker when their time is about to run out. Or when you video presentations, put one student in charge of filming."

Robert McLarty, teacher and author of *ETpedia Business English*

10 activities for last-minute substitutions with large classes

This final unit attempts to offer a few practical ideas and one-off activities that can be used on those difficult occasions when we are asked to substitute for a colleague at short notice, or to double-up our own class with another group at the last minute.

1. Use an accomplice to test students' memories

This activity involves a little bit of acting from the teacher, and also requires a willing accomplice. Before the lesson, find someone in the staffroom or school corridor who the students do not know. It might be a new colleague, a friend, or a visitor to the school. Ask them if they have 10 minutes to help you out. Ask your accomplice to wait near the classroom, out of the students' sight. Begin the lesson. Tell the students you have left something in the staffroom and that you will be right back. Leave the room. After a few seconds, send your accomplice in. Tell them to calmly steal a board marker from your desk before leaving the room again. Ask your accomplice to wait in the corridor. Wait a few moments before going back into the classroom on your own. As you re-enter the classroom, get the students' attention and ask them to copy down what you are going to write on the board. Look for your board marker. Pretend to be confused. Ask the students if they have seen it. The students – if they were paying attention – will tell you what just happened. Feign disbelief. Ask for a detailed description of the 'thief' – get students to write this down. As you compare answers, it will become apparent that the various eyewitness reports do not all match. This is the whole point of the activity – to demonstrate that everyone sees something different, and that eyewitness reports cannot necessarily be trusted. Now confess to the class what just happened. Open the door and invite your accomplice back in. Finally, get students to discuss what happened, and ask them to write a first-hand account of what happened, and how they felt.

2. Generate *Blockbusters* questions for a contest

Explain to students how to play *Blockbusters* (see Unit 33.6) and play a sample game on the board with two teams. Use general knowledge and vocabulary questions that you make up on the spot. Write a new grid on the board, complete with initial letters. Ask the students to come up with several questions for each letter and to write them down (with answers). Provide plenty of time, and encourage students to come up with as many possible questions as they can. When each group has generated at least two questions and answers for each letter on the board, begin the contest. Split the class into four groups: A, B, C and D. Team A plays team B using the questions generated by students from teams C and D, who are the question masters. Then teams C and D play each other in the second match, using the questions generated by teams A and B. Finally, hold the final game between the winners of the first two matches, using the same letters as before and with the questions being provided by the two teams that lost in the previous round. They can use up their unused questions from the first round.

3. Create a personal alphabet

Ask students to open their notebooks and write the English alphabet down the margin. Now ask them to choose a word for each letter of the alphabet that has some relevance to them and their lives. When they have finished, put students into pairs and ask them to compare lists. Their job is to guess why each particular word was chosen by their partner. As a follow-up, each student tries to memorise their partner's list, or to come up with a story involving as many of the words on their partner's list as they can.

4. Set puzzles and riddles

Build a collection of puzzles and riddles, or search for 'riddles' online. They will come in handy in these situations. Present students with a riddle and see if they can solve it. Allow them to ask questions, and provide hints if needed. There are three examples below. You might have time for several riddles. If there is any time remaining, invite students to share any riddles of their own, or get them to recall a scene from a TV programme or movie that featured a riddle or puzzle and to write down what the riddle was, and how it was solved.

Examples

	Puzzle	Solution
(i)	A B C D E F G ... P Q R S T U V W X Y Z	WATER (H to O → H_2O)
(ii)	A blind person can see it; a deaf person can hear it; but if they eat it, they will both die. What is it?	NOTHING
(iii)	Steve's dad has five sons. Their names are Ten, Twenty, Thirty, Forty and ...?	Steve

5. Write three-line dialogues

Give students a fixed phrase or phrase starter such as *It's not the kind of ....* Elicit ways in which the phrase can be used. Then get students into pairs and ask them to create a three-line dialogue incorporating that phrase. An example might be:

A: Nice hat!

B: Thanks. It's not the kind of thing I wear every day, but today is different.

A: How come?

When they have finished, students should agree on the context of their imagined dialogue, deciding who is speaking, where they are, and what the bigger picture is (in this case, why the speaker is wearing a hat). Then get volunteers to read out their dialogues. The others listen and ask questions and make guesses to discover the *who, where*, and *why* of each dialogue. Listen to several dialogues. Then repeat the activity with different pairings, using a slightly different fixed phrase, for example, *He's not the kind of ....* As an optional follow-up, invite students to extend each other's dialogues by adding more lines to them and then to perform them.

6. Generate Call My Bluff sentences

Put students into groups of three. Ask them to brainstorm some things that have happened to them recently – things that the others in the class do not know about. They do not have to be earth-shattering events. It could be a pleasant surprise (for example, *I found some money in the street last week*), a sighting (for example, *I saw the guy who presents the local TV news in the supermarket on Wednesday*) or a family incident (for example, *Last night my brother dropped my mum's phone and cracked the screen*). Each group should decide which one of the incidents to use. They say the chosen sentence in unison. Everyone in the group must pretend that the incident happened to them. The other students have the chance to ask questions. They then guess who was telling the truth. Students who guess correctly get a point. Continue the competition by listening to the next group.

7. True and false statements

Ask individual students to write three sentences about themselves, two of which are false and one of which is true. They should try to choose plausible lies and unlikely truths. Have a competition to see who can spot the most true sentences. Go round the class in turn. Each student reads out their three sentences. Get students to select which statement they think is true by raising their hand. Keep a track of the score as you go round the class.

8. Invent a reality-TV show

Write two columns on the board headed *Places in a Town* and *Abstract Nouns*. Elicit six examples for each column. Under *Places in a Town* you might get *bus station, supermarket, swimming pool, cinema* and *airport*. Under *Abstract Nouns*, you might get *truth, danger, happiness, friendship* and *democracy*. Now put students into pairs. Get them to choose one word from each column to make a compound noun, for example, *supermarket danger* or *airport democracy*. Now tell pairs that this is the title of a new reality TV show. They have to come up with the format of this imaginary programme, and explain it to the rest of the group. Students vote on which of the ideas sounds like it would make the best programme.

9. Significant numbers, places and names

Before class, think of two numbers that have some significance for you (for example, the number of years you have lived in your current apartment, the number of countries you have been to), two places that mean something to you (for example, where you were born, where you would like to go on holiday) and two significant names in your life (for example, your favourite cousin, your pet cat). Write the key numbers, places and names on the board, but do not explain why they are significant. Elicit guesses from students, and answer any follow-up questions that they might have. Then invite students to make their own list of two numbers, two places and two names. When they have finished, they work with a partner to discover the significance of each item on the list. Afterwards, ask students to write a short profile of their partner containing all the information revealed. Students change partners and repeat the task.

10. Dynamic dialogues

Divide the board into five sections, each one for a different part of speech. Label the sections (for example, *Adjectives*, *Verbs*, *Nouns*, *Adverbs* and *Prepositions*) and elicit examples of each. Put students into pairs and ask them to choose one word from each category. They then create a meaningful five-line dialogue with one of the five words in each line. Go round the class and listen to each of the dialogues. Invite students to comment on who they think the speakers are, and what the back story is in each case.

Appendix

Unit 6 sample questions to ask teenagers

1. What was your least favourite lesson last year? Why?

2. What was your favourite lesson last year? Why?

3. What would you like us to stop doing in English lessons? Why?

4. What would you like us to keep doing in English lessons? Why?

5. What do you think it would be worth trying out in English lessons? Why?

6. If you could choose, would you prefer to spend more time or less time learning English? Why?

7. Which is the hardest day of the week for you at school? Why?

8. What is your opinion of the homework you get?

9. What do you wish the teacher knew about you?

10. Is there anything you want to ask the teacher?

Unit 9.8: Sample listener roles for use in fishbowl discussions

Listening tasks for students in the outer circle.
(More than one student can take on any of these roles.)

Reporter Listen to the discussion as a reporter would. Take notes. Afterwards, write a short report about the discussion for those who were not there.

Micro-blogger Listen to the discussion and try to identify the opinions expressed by the different speakers. Summarise each speaker's main view in no more than 140 characters.

Voter Listen to the discussion and decide which speaker made the most convincing arguments. Make a note of any examples that seem particularly strong and explain why.

Language coach Before the discussion, choose one of the speakers to focus on. As you listen to the discussion, pay attention to how effectively your chosen speaker uses language. Afterwards, give them constructive feedback, looking at one of the following areas: grammar, vocabulary, pronunciation.

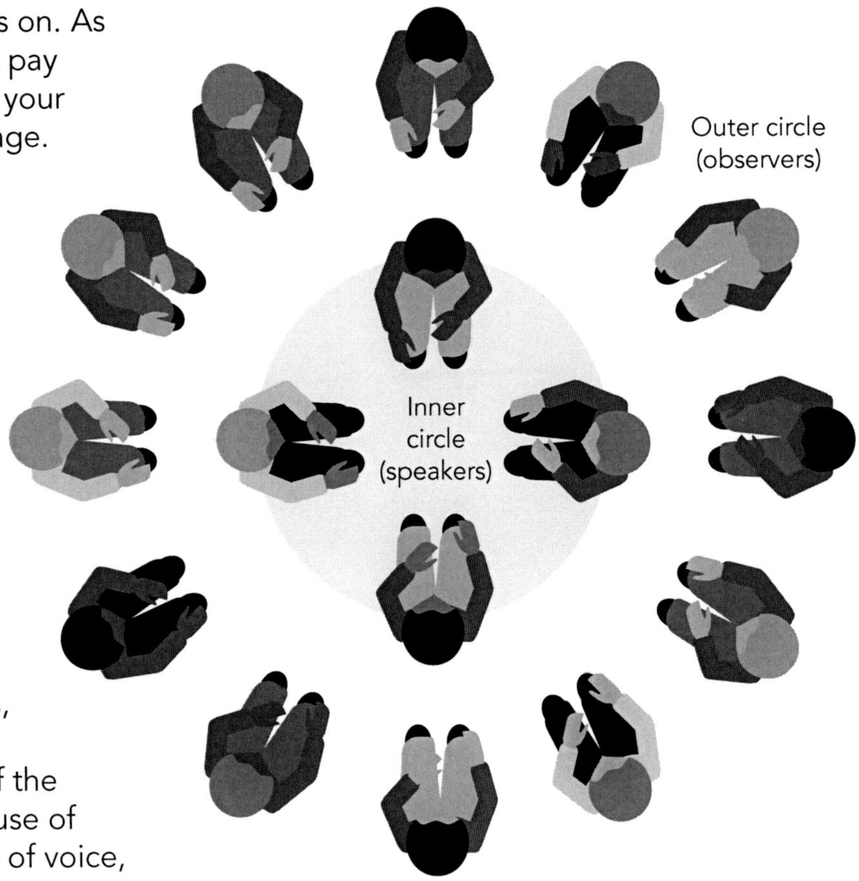

Communication coach Before the discussion, choose one of the speakers to focus on. As you listen to the discussion, pay attention to how well your chosen speaker is able to get their opinions across. Afterwards, give them constructive feedback, looking at one of the following areas: ideas and use of examples, delivery and use of voice, non-verbal communication.

Statistician Make a chart on a piece of paper with a column for each speaker. During the discussion, count how many contributions each speaker makes, and/or time how long they speak for. Afterwards, summarise the results and, with the teacher's guidance, invite speakers to say whether they felt they spoke too much, just enough, or not enough during the discussion.

Unit 14.10: Sample observation forms for student observers

1. Focused, structured observation

Class observed:	Date and time:
Name of observer:	
Focus of observation:	
What usually happens:	
What happened today:	
Key differences I noticed:	
My suggestions based on what I saw:	

2. Unfocused, structured observation

Class observed:	**Date and time:**
Name of observer:	
Focus of observation: Open – record any observations that you think are significant or interesting. Possible areas to consider: use of L1 by teacher and students, interaction between students in pairs and groups, on-task and off-task behaviour, use of different communicative skills (listening, reading, speaking, writing), use of the whiteboard, use of technology, teacher's movement around the room, questions asked by teacher, questions asked by students, correction methods used, or any general comments.	
Structure of observation: Focus on two students. Watch them throughout the lesson. Every five minutes, write down what is happening in the class at that moment and exactly what the two students are doing. Add any impressions or opinions that you have. 5′ 10′ 15′ 20′ 25′ 30′ 35′ 40′ 45′	
Other comments:	

Unit 16.6: Examples of paired cards for find-your-partner activities

Example sets below, based on the topic of instant messaging.

Question	Answer
What does ROFL mean?	Rolling on the floor laughing
What does SMH mean?	Shaking my head
What does TTYL mean?	Talk to you later
What does LOL mean?	Laughing out loud
What does NVM mean?	Never mind
What does TL;DR mean?	Too long; didn't read
What does BTW mean?	By the way
What does JK mean?	Just kidding
What does IRL mean?	In real life
What does OMG mean?	Oh my god

Word	Definition
Caps lock	After you press this button, every new letter will be in capitals
Gif	An animated image file
Emoji	A small image used to express an idea or an emotion in a text message
Netiquette	Rules of polite online behaviour
Username	A unique name or sequence of characters used to identify a user
#	The 'hashtag' symbol
@	The 'at' symbol
Snapchat	An image-messaging app with features such as 'Face Swap'
DM or PM	Direct message or private message
Group chat	A private online conversation between several people

Unit 31.7: Sample worksheet for the topic 'Decide what the headline should be'

Imagine you are the editors of the student newspaper at Radcliffe Secondary School. Look at the story below. It is going to appear in the newspaper.

Decide what the headline should be.

Think about your readers and come up with a headline containing the most relevant and eye-catching information for them.

Headline: ____

Teachers and students at Radcliffe Secondary School will be taking part in the Stay Safe Online Day planned for next Friday, 17 March, as part of Newton City Council's Internet Safety Awareness Day. Workshops and presentations led by internet-safety experts will take place in the school's award-winning auditorium, starting with a talk at 9am by local TV presenter Lesley North. Radcliffe Secondary headteacher Simon Day said, 'This is an important topic for both teachers and students, so I would be delighted if everyone was able to attend the whole-day event. I am grateful to the school staff for agreeing to rearrange their daily schedules, and am sure that the exams originally planned for 17 March can be rescheduled later in the month'.

Unit 33.2: Sample worksheet for extreme cloze contest (1 of 3)

Student worksheet:

Find the missing words to complete the text.

Facebook: a teenager's view

'Facebook is useful for [1]________ [2]________ [3]________ [4]________ finding
[5]________ [6]________ [7]________, but [8]________ [9]________ [10]________.
No-one really [11]________ [12]________ [13]________ any more. [14]________
too [15]________. [16]________ [17]________ Instagram. [18]________ [19]________
casual, [20]________ you can [21]________ [22]________ [23]________ [24]________
[25]________. [26]________ [27]________ [28]________ way [29]________ [30]________
yourself. Actually, I think [31]________ [32]________ Facebook [33]________
[34]________ [35]________ [36]________. [37]________ mean, [38]________ [39]________
[40]________, [41]________ [42]________ generally [43]________ [44]________.
[45]________ [46]________ other people's [47]________ [48]________ [49]________
comments. [50]________ [51]________ really [52]________ [53]________ any more.
[54]________ [55]________ bit unusual [56]________ [57]________ [58]________ age
[59]________ [60]________ [61]________ [62]________ Facebook.'

Linda, 17, Hungary

Unit 33.2: Sample worksheet for extreme cloze contest (2 of 3)

Teacher's key

Use this alphabetical chart to respond to students' guesses. For example, if the word guessed is ***they***, you can quickly check the chart to see that the word ***they*** appears twice – in gaps 38 and 45. Award two points to the students who guessed correctly, and allow all the students to fill in the two gaps on their worksheet.

a	22, 27, 55, 60
about	6
active	44
and	4, 20, 41, 48
anything	12
are	42
be	21
chatting	1
cool	10, 28
creative	25
do	36, 52
don't	51
events	7
express	30
formal	15
friends	3
I	37
if	56
it's	8, 14, 18, 26, 54

leave	49
lot	23, 61
more	19, 24, 33, 40, 43
my	58
not	9
on	62
out	5
parents	31
post	39
posts	11, 47, 59
read	46
someone	57
than	34
that	53
there	13
they	38, 45
to	2, 29
use	17, 32
we	16, 35, 50

Unit 33.2: Sample worksheet for extreme cloze contest (3 of 3)

Master version

Once the activity is underway, this allows you to see at a glance which words are still missing. Every time there is a correct guess, cross off or circle the numbers corresponding to the words guessed. If students get stuck, you might want to give them a hint. The master version shows you which words are still missing. The words in **bold** are the words that are already provided in the student's worksheet, and so do not have to be guessed.

Facebook: a teenager's view

'Facebook is useful for [1] chatting [2] to [3] friends [4] and **finding**
[5] out [6] about [7] events **, but** [8] it's [9] not [10] cool**.**
No-one really [11] posts [12] anything [13] there **any more.** [14] It's
too [15] formal**.** [16] We [17] use **Instagram.** [18] It's [19] more
casual, [20] and **you can** [21] be [22] a [23] lot [24] more
[25] creative**.** [26] It's [27] a [28] cool **way** [29] to [30] express
yourself. Actually, I think [31] parents [32] use **Facebook** [33] more
[34] than [35] we [36] do**.** [37] I **mean,** [38] they [39] post
[40] more**,** [41] and [42] are **generally** [43] more [44] active**.**
[45] They [46] read **other people's** [47] posts [48] and [49] leave
comments. [50] We [51] don't **really** [52] do [53] that **any more.**
[54] It's [55] a **bit unusual** [56] if [57] someone [58] my **age**
[59] posts [60] a [61] lot [62] on **Facebook.'**

Linda, 17, Hungary

Complete text:

Facebook: a teenager's view

'Facebook is useful for chatting to friends and finding out about events, but it's not cool. No-one really posts anything there any more. It's too formal. We use Instagram. It's more casual, and you can be a lot more creative. It's a cool way to express yourself. Actually, I think parents use Facebook more than we do. I mean, they post more, and are generally more active. They read other people's posts and leave comments. We don't really do that any more. It's a bit unusual if someone my age posts a lot on Facebook.'

Linda, 17, Hungary

Unit 33.6: Sample grid for Blockbusters game

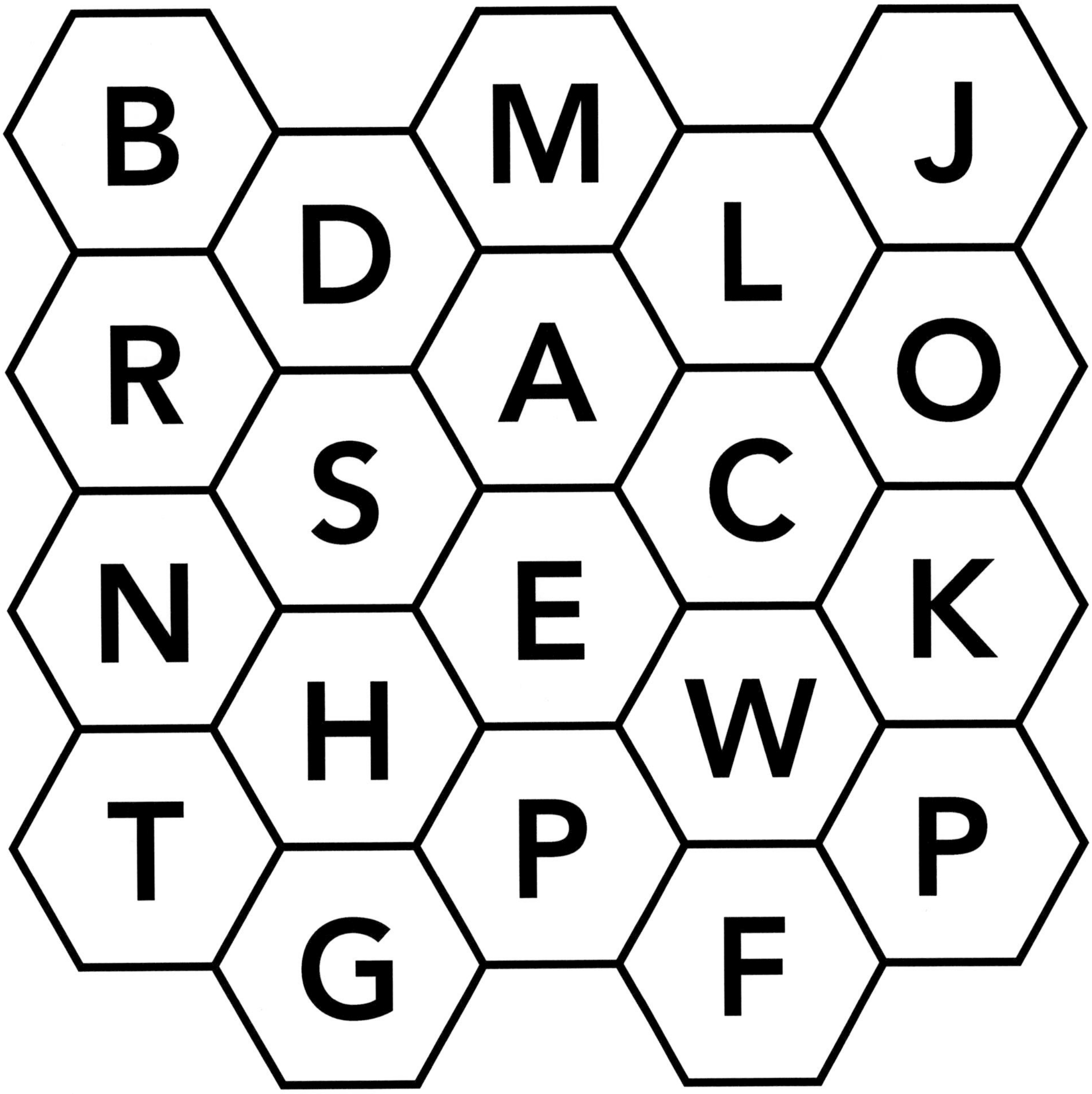

Unit 34.6: Sample flowchart with grammar reference and exercise

Grammar reference: *too* and *enough*

1. We use *too* and *enough* to talk about how too much of something or too little of something prevented something from happening:
   too + adjective + infinitive: *I was* ***too slow to win*** *the race.*
   not + adjective + *enough* + infinitive: *I was**n't fast enough to win*** *the race.*

2. Note the word order with *enough*:
   enough + noun: *We didn't have* ***enough money*** *to eat out.*
   adjective + *enough*: *The restaurants weren't* ***cheap enough*** *to eat out.*

Practice exercise:

Complete the sentences with **too** or **enough**.

1. The hat is ______________ expensive to buy.
2. These shoes aren't big ______________ to wear.
3. We haven't got ______________ time to see the movie.
4. It isn't warm ______________ to eat ice cream.
5. The box is ______________ heavy to lift.

Flowchart

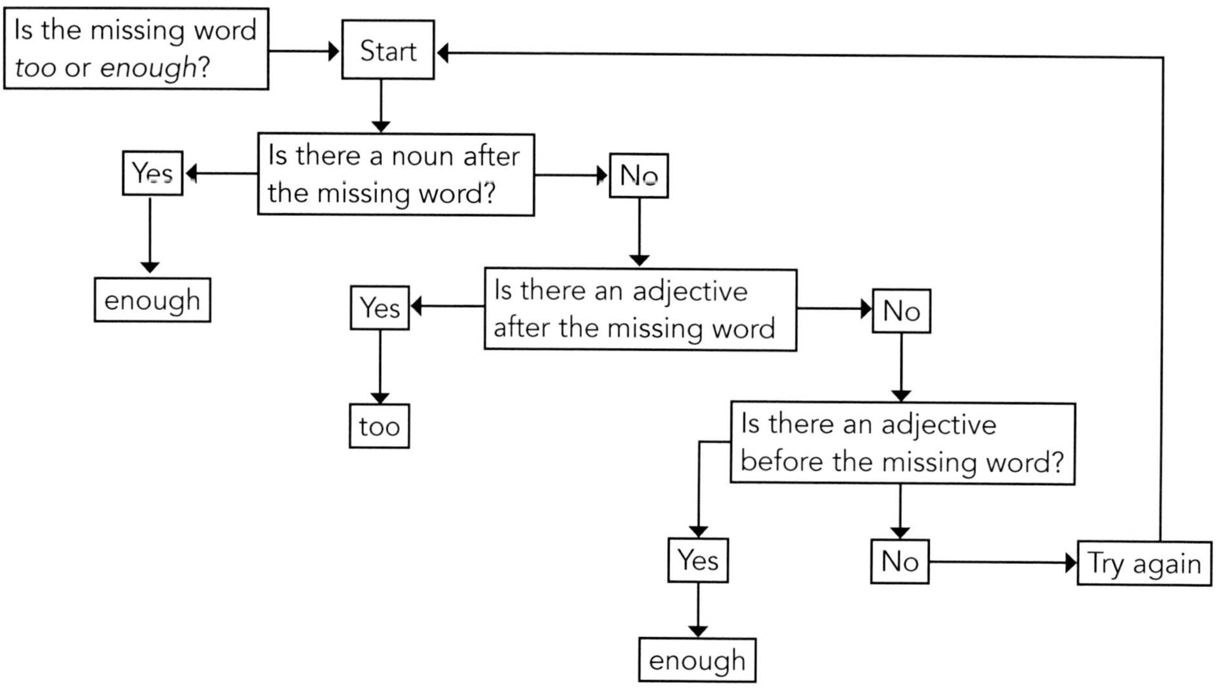

Unit 35.10: Sample list of teacher's correction codes

WO *you also can*	incorrect word order
made of a paper	not needed here
Physics difficult	something is missing
She's gonna call	style is inappropriate here
I getting up at six	wrong tense
They didn't finishing	grammar mistake
The test was heavy	wrong vocabulary
Satisfaction guarantied	problem with spelling or punctuation
Cook here not	meaning is not clear

Write your own 10 tips

Do you have 10 more ideas for English language teachers? Then why not write them down and share them with your colleagues or share them on the My ETpedia blog at www.myetpedia.com?

1. ....

2. ....

3. ....

4. ....

5. ....

Write your own 10 tips

6. ....

....

....

....

....

7. ....

....

....

....

....

8. ....

....

....

....

....

9. ....

....

....

....

....

10. ....

....

....

....

....

Introduction

Proof reading is an essential part of written English – and the hardest work to proof read is your own. Therefore these sheets will hopefully enable children to develop skills by proof reading the work of others.

The mistakes within the passages are not random, but specifically related to the work covered in *Spelling Made Easy*, from the Introductory Level to Level 2. Following the marking, both teachers and children will be aware of word families, individual words and aspects of punctuation which need to be re-taught and reinforced. The children might also have been reminded that punctuation is part of meaning. Through the absence of full stops or question marks, the reader has been unsure of the intended meaning of the writer.

For some children, the following guidelines might be helpful in connection with *Be The Teacher*, but also with their own written work.

<u>Guidelines</u>

(a) Read through the passage aloud for meaning. Do not let the eyes just glide over it.

(b) Read with a pencil/ball point pen in the hand, following each word as it is read. This will help the student to spot words that have been omitted because the voice alone may put these in and the eyes will be deceived.

(c) The voice and the pencil will falter if the punctuation is wrong. Punctuation is a vital part of meaning.

(d) Re-read for spelling errors. Hopefully, warning bells will ring over wrong spellings and misuse of words. Even if corrections cannot be made, the spotting of errors is a good sign and should be encouraged.

As the mistakes are not their own but those of the pupils of Brand's Patch School, the children will hopefully enjoy the work and will become increasingly aware of their own weaknesses.

The weaknesses of individual children will be revealed by the corrections that are not in red!

PROOF READING ACTIVITIES

PHOTOCOPIABLE MASTERS

BE THE
TEACHER
BOOK
1

Spelling Made Easy SERIES

Corresponding to Spelling Made Easy
Introductory Level and Level 1

Best Selling Series by

Violet Brand

Published by BrandBooks

England

Be the Teacher Book One. First published in the United Kingdom in 1996
by Egon Publishers Ltd.

ISBN 1 899998 02 0

(10 digit ISBN 1-904421-08-3

13 digit ISBN 978-1-904421-085

Index

Introduction for the Brand's Patch School teachers

You are now the teachers at Brand's Patch School and you will have to mark the pieces of work that the children write. Like all teachers, you can use a red pencil (or ball point pen).

Some of the children will make spelling mistakes. Will you spot all of the words they get wrong? Will you be able to write the words correctly with your red pen? Will you notice the speech marks and capital letters that are missing?

Remember, if full stops or question marks are left out, you might be puzzled about what the writer is trying to say.

When you have finished your marking with the red pen, you will probably want to know whether you spotted all of the mistakes. Your teacher will give you another sheet of the same work, with the corrections made.

The question is, were there any mistakes you missed?

1. Martin Andrews   Munday, September 15th

Wen we was coming to school on the trane, a boy snached my sachel. he draged it along the door and jumpd out wen the trane stoped.

i ran to the door and shoutd, Stop him! Stop him!

i saw him ran up the steps whith my sachel. the doors shut and the trane startd.

I know my famly will be very cros. sachels cost a lot of mony.

Monday,
1. Martin Andrews Munday, September 15th

When were train, snatched
Wen we was coming to school on the trane, a boy snached

satchel. He dragged to jumped when
my sachel. he draged it along ^ the door and jumpd out wen the

train stopped.
trane stoped.

I shouted
i ran to the door and shoutd, "Stop him! Stop him!"

I run with satchel. The
i saw him ran up the steps whith my sachel. the doors shut

train started.
and the trane startd.

family cross. Satchels money.
I know my famly will be very cros. sachels cost a lot of mony.

Did you miss any mistakes?

Did you notice all of the mistakes that Martin made? If not, think hard about those you missed.

Then take another coloured pencil (not red) and make the corrections. Hopefully, you will not make the same mistakes yourself.

Remind yourself of the 'tch' family, if these were some of the words you overlooked.

2. Jane Brown Tuseday, september 23rd

My farther was knoked down when he went joging larst nite. he was trying to doge a car that zomed across the zeba crosing, but he was not farst enuff. He was draged along the rode until the car shot away. my dads bos was in the next car and he helped him up. He taked him to the hosptal. Dads in their whith tow broken legs. He is very cros whith the driver woh did not stop.

Tuesday, September

2. Jane Brown Tuseday, september 23rd

---

father knocked when jogging last night.

My farther was knoked down when he went joging larst nite.

He dodge zoomed zebra crossing,

he was trying to doge a car that zomed across the zeba crosing,

fast enough. dragged road

but he was not farst enuff. He was draged along the rode until

My dad's boss

the car shot away. my dads bos was in the next car and he

took hospital. Dad's there with

helped him up. He taked him to the hosptal. Dads in their whith

two cross with who

tow broken legs. He is very cros whith the driver woh did not

stop.

Did you miss any mistakes?

Jane must be worried about her father and she certainly made quite a few spelling mistakes when she wrote about his accident.

Did you spot them all?

If there were any you missed, think hard about them and make the corrections with your other coloured pencil (not red).

3. Laura Cook Wednesday, October 1st

24 brige road

brand's pach

febuary 20

dere gran,

Thank you very much for the chrismas presnt. sorry Im a bit late wiv this letter, but the techer give us lots of homework to do in the holidays.

larst nite it was the shool disco, witch was lots of fun untill I triped over and broke my rist. The techer phond dad who came in his mincab. He taked me to the Distrit Hospital were we had to wate for ages to sea a docter.

I broke my rite rist, but I right with my left hand, so I don't have to sit in shool and do nuthing,

Luv

Laura xxxx

3. Laura Cook Wednesday, October 1st

Bridge Road
24 brige road
Brand's Patch
brand's pach
February 20th
febuary 20

Dear Gran,
dere gran,

Christmas present. Sorry I'm
Thank you very much for the chrismas presnt. sorry Im a bit
with teacher gave
late wiv this letter, but the techer give us lots of homework to do

in the holidays.

Last night school which until
larst nite it was the shool disco, witch was lots of fun untill I
tripped wrist. teacher phoned Dad
triped over and broke my rist. The techer phond dad who came
minicab. took District where
in his mincab. He taked me to the Distrit Hospital were we had to
wait see doctor.
wate for ages to sea a docter.

right wrist, write
I broke my rite rist, but I right with my left hand, so I don't
school nothing.
have to sit in shool and do nuthing,

Love
Luv

Laura xxxx

Did you miss any mistakes?

I wonder what Laura's Gran thought when she saw all the mistakes in Laura's letter?

But I am sure she was still <u>very</u> pleased to receive it.

Did you notice all of the mistakes? If not think hard about those you missed and then correct them with your other coloured pencil (not red).

4. Alex Driver thursday, october 9th

Hour clars went to the Electronik Show on the Embankmant on wenesday. Tow other clarses came, so there was sevnty of us. Some mothers and farthers came to.

We didn't know what to expet, but it was relly good. their were lots of trade stands whith eletronic things we culd construt, or just try out. None of it felt like school.

We was wating at the ext to go and cach the trane home, when the fire warning went off. The techers got us out farst before the hundrds of other people got to the ext.

It was hetic four us, but I spect it was much worse for the others left insid.

Thursday, October

4\. Alex Driver thursday, october 9th

Our class Electronic Embankment

Hour clars went to the Electronik Show on the Embankmant

Wednesday. Two classes were seventy

on wenesday. Tow other clarses came, so there was sevnty of us.

fathers too.

Some mothers and farthers came to.

expect, really There

We didn't know what to expet, but it was relly good. their

with electronic could construct,

were lots of trade stands whith eletronic things we culd construt,

or just try out. None of it felt like school.

were waiting exit catch train

We was wating at the ext to go and cach the trane home,

teachers fast

when the fire warning went off. The techers got us out farst

hundreds exit.

before the hundrds of other people got to the ext.

hectic for expect

It was hetic four us, but I spect it was much worse for the

inside.

others left insid.

Did you miss any mistakes?

When fire alarms go off it can be very frightening – even if there is really no fire!

Did you notice all of the mistakes, especially those in the 'e' family? Think carefully about those you missed and then correct them.

5. Sam Elton — Friday, October 10th

Who is the culpret arsked the Headmarster. Over one hundrid childrn were silent. the hall was quite as they sit waiting for a hand to up.

Ill arsk agen sed the Headmarster. Who is the culpret Who took mr browns trumpit and through it over the hege

No hand went up.

Right said the Head. You are all supect and so there will be no playtime for eny of you. You will go to all lesons, then at break-tim, you will come and sit this floor. Do you undstand

Yes sir said the childrn very quitely.

5. Sam Elton Friday, October 10th

culprit?" asked Headmaster.
"Who is the culpret arsked the Headmarster. Over one
hundred children The quiet sat
hundrid childrn were silent. the hall was quite as they sit waiting
go
for a hand to ^ up.
"I'll ask again," said Headmaster. culprit?
Ill arsk agen sed the Headmarster. "Who is the culpret?
Mr Brown's trumpet threw hedge?"
Who took mr browns trumpit and through it over the hege

No hand went up.

suspect
"Right," said the Head. "You are all supect and so there will be
any lessons,
no playtime for eny of you. You will go to all lesons, then at
break-time, on understand?"
break-tim, you will come and sit ^ this floor. Do you undstand
children quietly.
"Yes sir," said the childrn very quitely.

Did you miss any mistakes?

I wonder who did take Mr Brown's trumpet and how many playtimes the children had to lose until he or she told the Head?.

Did you miss any mistakes? What about the speech marks? Think hard and correct those you did not spot.

6. Jessica Frame Monday, October 20th

Our knew class projeckt this term is on rivers. We are allowed to chose one burd or animal that lifes in the river or on the river bak to right about for home work.

I have choosed ducks.

Their is about 115 diffrent kinds of ducks in the world. There necks is much short than the neks of swons and they all have webed foot.

The female ducks is dull colours, but they is good muthers to the ducklins. The male ducks does not sit on the eggs and does not hlp to look after the babys when they hach.

Monday,

6. Jessica Frame Monday, October 20th

---

new project
Our knew class projeckt this term is on rivers. We are allowed
choose bird lives
to chose one burd or animal that lifes in the river or on the river
bank write homework.
bak to right about for home work.

chosen
I have choosed ducks.

There are different Their
Their is about 115 diffrent kinds of ducks in the world. There
are shorter necks swans
necks is much short than the neks of swons and they all have
webbed feet.
webed foot.

are coloured are mothers
The female ducks is dull colours, but they is good muthers to
ducklings. do do
the ducklins. The male ducks does not sit on the eggs and does
help babies hatch.
not hlp to look after the babys when they hach.

Did you miss any mistakes?

Jessica did not get everything right, as I am sure you have noticed.

If you missed any mistakes, correct with your other pencil (not red) and think hard.

7. Ian Gibbs Teusday, November 2nd

When we went home fom school yestday the slet was startin to fall. their was a stong breez.

Its cold my mother said. Put your hands you jaket poket to keep them warm.

Im O.K. I wont freez, I said to her. Im not a baby. Im tuff. But I did sqeeze my hands up my sleevs.

When we got home, we had a hot cup of coffe and a chees sanwich. We had just finshed when we herd a sceech of braks outsid.

It were my big brother.

Your early said Mum.

The boss thort it was goin to freez, so he sent us home early, he told her.

Tuesday,

7. Ian Gibbs — Teusday, November 2nd

---

from yesterday sleet starting
When we went home fom school yestday the slet was startin
There strong breeze
to fall. their was a stong breez.

"It's in your jacket pockets
Its cold," my mother said. "Put your hands ^ you jaket poket
to keep them warm."

"I'm won't freeze "I'm I'm tough."
Im O.K. I wont freez," I said to her. Im not a baby. Im tuff.
squeeze sleeves.
But I did sqeeze my hands up my sleevs.

coffee cheese
When we got home, we had a hot cup of coffe and a chees
sandwich. finished heard screech brakes
sanwich. We had just finshed when we herd a sceech of braks
outside.
outsid.

was
It were my big brother.

"You're
"Your early," said Mum.

thought going freeze,
"The boss thort it was goin to freez, so he sent us home
early," he told her.

Did you miss any mistakes?

That was kind of the boss, wasn't it? Did you spot Ian's mistakes with the 'ee' words and that he forgot speech marks?

Think carefully about the mistakes you missed and then correct them with your pencil (not red).

8. Katy Hicks Wensday, November 3rd

Son it will be Guy Fawkes Night and our mother and farther sed we must chose were we would like to go for our fireworks. We looked each uther, but my bruther and I couldn't chose.

He was mody and lookd gloom. I felt folish.

My muther said, Come on. Mack up your minds. The tea's nealy cookd.

My farther bomed. "Write. Well go to the park.

I flt folish, but my bother sed, "That's what I was going to say.

He had stoped looking glomy and began smile.

I agred with him and thort "I bet that's where his frend is going."

Wednesday,

8. Katy Hicks Wensday, November 3rd

Soon father

Son it will be Guy Fawkes Night and out mother and farther

said choose where

sed we must chose were we would like to go for our fireworks.

at other, brother choose.

We looked ^ each uther, but my bruther and I couldn't chose.

moody looked gloomy. foolish.

He was mody and lookd gloom. I felt folish.

mother Make

My muther said, Come on. Mack up your minds. The tea's

nearly cooked."

nealy cookd.

father boomed, "Right. We'll park!"

My farther bomed. "Write. Well go to the park.

felt foolish brother said,

I flt folish, but my bother sed, "That's what I was going to

say."

stopped gloomy to

He had stoped looking glomy and began ^ smile.

agreed thought friend

I agred with him and thort "I bet that's where his frend is

going."

Did you miss any mistakes?

I think Katy had better look carefully at the words in the 'oo' family again.

Did you notice all of her mistakes? If there were any you did not spot, think carefully, then correct. You do not want to make the same mistakes in your own writing do you?

9. Gary Inward — Friday, November 5th

This is November 5th and so its Guy Fawkes Night. as son as its drk Dad will cum home form the markt, Mum will come form the carpt shop and we'll have tea. after tea we will leave the washing-up and go the Comon to sea the big bonfire wiv Guy Fawkes on top.

Then thay will strt the fireworks. The ligts and bags will go off all across the Comon. Wot a row! The fireworks can't do any harm, but somtimes I fel a bit frightned.

9. Gary Inward — Friday, November 5th

it's — As soon
This is November 5th and so its Guy Fawkes Night. as son as
it's dark — come — from — market, — from
its drk Dad will cum home form the markt, Mum will come form
carpet — After
the carpt shop and we'll have tea. after tea we will leave the
to — Common — see — with
washing-up and go ^ the Comon to sea the big bonfire wiv Guy
Fawkes on top.

they — start — lights — bangs
Then thay will strt the fireworks. The ligts and bags will go off
across — Common. What — can't
all across the Comon. Wot a row! The fireworks can't do any
sometimes feel — frightened.
harm, but somtimes I fel a bit frightned.

Did you miss any mistakes?

Do you sometimes feel frightened of fireworks? If you do, you probably do not tell your friends

Gary did get the date right. But did you notice his other mistakes and correct them?

10. Katy Hicks Munday, November 8th

We had rarther a shok on Guy Fawkes Nite. We was standing in the prk wiv hundrds of others waiting for the bonfire to start wen, all of a suden, their was a big flash and the groud startd shakeing.

I began to shuder. The bonfire strted with another big flash, then rokets zomed into the sky and hundrds of spaklers strted flashing. Polis alrms were boming out and a loud vice shoutd

Don't panic Don't panic

There were anuther big crash and lots of rockets zomed of. I was shakeing. I put my hands in my jaket pokets and stod whith my eyes shut tigt.

My father said. We must go home. We must not stay in the park.

I was glad and so were my bruther.

Monday,

10. Katy Hicks Munday, November 8th

---

rather shock Night. were
We had rarther a shok on Guy Fawkes Nite. We was standing
park with hundreds
in the prk wiv hundrds of others waiting for the bonfire to start
when, sudden, there ground started
wen, all of a suden, their was a big flash and the groud startd
shaking.
shakeing.

shudder. started
I began to shuder. The bonfire strted with another big flash,
rockets zoomed hundreds sparklers started
then rokets zomed into the sky and hundrds of spaklers strted
Police alarms booming voice shouted,
flashing. Polis alrms were boming out and a loud vice shoutd
panic! panic!"
"Don't panic Don't panic

was another zoomed off.
There were anuther big crash and lots of rockets zomed of. I
shaking jacket pockets stood with
was shakeing. I put my hands in my jaket pokets and stod whith
tight.
my eyes shut tigt.

My father said. "We must go home. We must not stay in the park."

was brother.
I was glad and so were my bruther.

Did you miss any mistakes?

This is Katy Hicks writing some more about Bonfire Night. She may have been sorry that they chose to go to the park.

She still cannot spell brother. Did you notice her mistake? If you missed it again, think very hard before you correct it. Also think hard about any others you did not spot.

11. Helen Jones — Wensday, November 10th

Larst yere we was the champon under-twlve net-ball team and we was on the Channl 4 News wen we one the larst mach. Next weak we strt the comptition agen.

Their have bin quiet a few changs in the team four this yere. Lots of the girls have left and gone to secondary schol. I think I'm going to be the shoter and my frend is the gaol keper. But the teacher keps changeing us around, so we don't quiet no wot to expet next.

We chater about the changes at luch time to sea if we can sort out woh is best in each place. Then we finish up just chaseing each other roud the play-ground. We've agred that the teacher will chose the team. It's hour job to win the mach and the champonship.

Wednesday,

11. Helen Jones Wensday, November 10th

Last year were champion under-twelve netball
Larst yere we was the champon under-twlve net-ball team
were Channel when won last match.
and we was on the Channl 4 News wen we one the larst mach.
week start competition again.
Next weak we strt the comptition agen.
There been quite changes for year.
Their have bin quiet a few changs in the team four this yere.
school.
Lots of the girls have left and gone to secondary schol. I think
shooter friend goal keeper.
I'm going to be the shoter and my frend is the gaol keper. But
keeps changing quite know what
the teacher keps changeing us around, so we don't quiet no wot
expect
to expet next.
chatter lunch-time see
We chater about the changes at luch time to sea if we can
who
sort out woh is best in each place. Then we finish up just
chasing round playground agreed
chaseing each other roud the play-ground. We've agred that the
choose our match
teacher will chose the team. It's hour job to win the mach and
championship.
the champonship.

Did you miss any mistakes?

Did you manage to correct all of Helen's mistakes? If so, well done!

Look carefully at those you missed, think hard and then correct them with your coloured pencil (not red).

12. Paul Kingston Monday, Nov. 15th

Wen we was comeing to school this morning, my friend throw a hrd ball at me and it hit my thum. I thort my thum was brokn. the school nurs see it and said it wasn't, but she thort it wuld still hert a lot.

In arithmtic we had a test. the techer red out numbers and we had to right them. I thik I got them write. I'll know on tuseday wen we get the tests back.

This is wot I wrote –

forth, fith, sixh, therd, sevnth, thousnd.

Is they riht?

November

12. Paul Kingston Monday, Nov. 15th

When were coming threw
Wen we was comeing to school this morning, my friend throw
hard thumb. thought thumb broken.
a hrd ball at me and it hit my thum. I thort my thum was brokn.
The nurse saw thought would
the school nurs see it and said it wasn't, but she thort it wuld
hurt
still hert a lot.

arithmetic The teacher read
In arithmtic we had a test. the techer red out numbers and we
write think right. Tuesday
had to right them. I thik I got them write. I'll know on tuseday
when
wen we get the tests back.

what
This is wot I wrote –

fourth, fifth, sixth, third, seventh, thousand.
forth, fith, sixh, therd, sevnth, thousnd.

Are right?
Is they riht?

Did you miss any mistakes?

Well – are they? Did Paul get any of them right? Were you able to correct his mistakes?

If you missed any, think very hard then write the right words with your coloured pencil (not red).

13. Virginia Lake Teusday, Novmber 16th

I have bin playing the rcorder four for years but now I'm getting bord whith it.

Can I play the trumpit I arsked my mother.

Grils don't play trumpits," she sed wiv a snort.

Thay do, I said. "The docter's gril does. She's in my class.

Arsk yor father," Mum orderd. "I've got more importnt things than trumpits to thing about. We've got visiters comeing to supper

Who" I asked.

A sailer and his wife. Come on. You can help instead of standing their chatering about trumpits.

I did hlp her. We had just finished when Dad came with the visiters.

The most importnt thing I find out wen we was haveing super was that the sailer's wife plays the trumpit!

Tuesday, November 16th

13. Virginia Lake Teusday, Novmber 16th

been recorder for four
I have bin playing the rcorder four for years but now I'm

bored with
getting bord whith it.

trumpet?" asked
"Can I play the trumpit I arsked my mother.

"Girls trumpets," said with
Grils don't play trumpits," she sed wiv a snort.

"They doctor's girl
Thay do," I said. "The docter's gril does. She's in my class."

"Ask your ordered. important
Arsk yor father," Mum orderd. "I've got more importnt things

trumpets think visitors coming
than trumpits to thing about. We've got visiters comeing to

supper

"Who?" I asked.

sailor
"A sailer and his wife. Come on. You can help instead of

there chattering trumpets."
standing their chatering about trumpits.

help
I did hlp her. We had just finished when Dad came with the

visitors.
visiters.

important found when were having supper
The most importnt thing I find out wen we was haveing super

sailor's trumpet!
was that the sailer's wife plays the trumpit!

Did you make any mistakes?

That was Virginia's lucky evening, I think. Perhaps she is now playing the trumpet. I hope she can spell the name of the instrument correctly.

Did you spot her mistakes? Did you also notice her other errors? If you missed any, look carefully, think hard and make the corrections.

14. Nigel Morgan Wenesday, Novmber 17th

The pavment in our road was damagd last night when some stragers had a car rase. Won of them was going so fast that he crashd into a shop widow. Too other cars hit him. What a mess! They was very luky that none of them were killed.

Soon the road was full of ambulances and police cars. The noise and all those bloo lights flashing woke me up – and everone else in the steet. I looked out of my bedrom widow and saw them takeing the drives away on stretchers. My parnts think that they did not have there safty belts on.

After all that it take me a long to get back to sleep.

Wednesday, November

14. Nigel Morgan Wenesday, Novmber 17th

---

pavement damaged

The pavment in our road was damagd last night when some

strangers race. One

stragers had a car rase. Won of them was going so fast that he

crashed window. Two

crashd into a shop widow. Too other cars hit him. What a mess!

were lucky

They was very luky that none of them were killed.

Soon the road was full of ambulances and police cars. The

blue

noise and all those bloo lights flashing woke me up – and

everyone street. bedroom window

everone else in the steet. I looked out of my bedrom widow and

taking drivers parents

saw them takeing the drives away on stretchers. My parnts think

their safety

that they did not have there safty belts on.

took time

After all that it take me a long ∧ to get back to sleep.

Did you miss any mistakes?

Nigel was probably tired after the disturbance last night. He did not make too many mistakes.

Did you notice them all? If there were any you missed, correct them now, thinking carefully.

15. Ann McNab Thursday, November 18th

My Great Grandma was ninty on Teusday and my brother was ninteen. There where two partys. Won for Great Grandma at tea-tim and another four my brother at super-time.

I had to play Hapy Brithday for Great Grandma on my flut and my brothers played it on the trumpit. Everone else sing.

Mum had made a large choclate cake for her with ninty candles. We all helpd her to blew them out. My brother had ice-crem cake. We had to blew the ninteen candles out qickly before they meltd that cake.

I had a little bit of cake and then had to bed a long time before his frends went.

That is I am much young than them.

15. Ann McNab Thursday, November 18th

---

ninety Tuesday
My Great Grandma was ninty on Teusday and my brother was
nineteen. were parties, one
ninteen. There where two partys. Won for Great Grandma at
tea-time for supper-time.
tea-tim and another four my brother at super-time.

Happy Birthday flute
I had to play Hapy Brithday for Great Grandma on my flut
trumpet. Everyone sang.
and my brothers played it on the trumpit. Everone else sing.

chocolate ninety
Mum had made a large choclate cake for her with ninty
helped blow an
candles. We all helpd her to blew them out. My brother had ∧
cream blow nineteen quickly
ice-crem cake. We had to blew the ninteen candles out qickly
melted
before they meltd that cake.

go to
I had a little bit of cake and then had to ∧ bed a long time
friends
before his frends went.

because younger
That is ∧ I am much young than them.

Did you miss any mistakes?

Ann got the date right. Did she follow with a perfect piece of writing? Not quite perfect, I think.

Did you notice all her mistakes and correct them? If not, think hard about those you missed and correct them now.

16. Bill Newton — Friday, November 19th

My parnts had some friend staying last weeknd and they both kept smokeing. I kept chocking because I am not used to haveing people in the house what smock.

On monday they left go to stay in a Londun hotle. I heard my mother phoneing her sistr. She was teling her about the hole house smeling of smok

Evn our cloths smell she expoded.

When my father came home from work he said, Im going to put a notise on our front door that seys, SMOKEING is FORBIDEN inside this house.

Good for you said Mum. We all agree.

16. Bill Newton Friday, November 19th

parents friends weekend
My parnts had some friend staying last weeknd and they both
smoking. choking having
kept smokeing. I kept chocking because I am not used to haveing
who smoke.
people in the house what smock.

Monday to London hotel.
On monday they left ^ go to stay in a Londun hotle. I heard
phoning sister. telling whole
my mother phoneing her sistr. She was teling her about the hole
smelling smoke.
house smeling of smok

"Even clothes exploded.
Evn our cloths smell," she expoded.

"I'm
When my father came home from work he said, Im going to
notice says SMOKING FORBIDDEN
put a notise on our front door that seys, SMOKEING is FORBIDEN
inside this house."

"Good for you" said Mum. "We all agree."

Did you miss any mistakes?

Bill still does not know words in the 'o-e' family. He will need to look hard at that family again and read the words aloud, noticing the 'tricky bits' within them.

Did you spot all of his mistakes? If not, correct them now (not with a red pencil) and then look at the 'o-e' family again. What about other mistakes?.

17. Jill Owen Monday, November 22th

On Saterday my dads rugger team had a fixter ninty mile away. Because my mother and brother wanted to go, I had to go to. I couldn't thing of any xcuse not to and my mother woud not let me stay at home alon.

Now I am glad did go because their was some ruff playing and my father was injered. He was took off on a stretcher and then they him to hosptal. We followed in the car. I sat with my mother the frunt and I could see her hands and legs shakeing as she was driveing along.

The team of docter thort that Dad had damiged his spine. We was all very quite until the docters at the hospital sed that it was not his spine, but muscles in back. Dad has to stay four for days, so Mum will fetch him tomorrow

17. Jill Owen — Monday, November 22th

Saturday Dad's fixture ninety miles
On Saterday my dads rugger team had a fixter ninty mile

away. Because my mother and brother wanted to go, I had to go
too think excuse would
to. I couldn't thing of any xcuse not to and my mother woud not
alone.
let me stay at home alon.

I there rough
Now I am glad ^ did go because their was some ruff playing
injured. taken
and my father was injered. He was took off on a stretcher and
took hospital.
then they ^ him to hosptal. We followed in the car. I sat with my
in front shaking
mother ^ the frunt and I could see her hands and legs shakeing as
driving
she was driveing along.

doctors thought damaged
The team of docter thort that Dad had damiged his spine. We
were quiet doctors said
was all very quite until the docters at the hospital sed that it was
his for four
not his spine, but muscles in ^ back. Dad has to stay four for

days, so Mum will fetch him tomorrow

Did you miss any mistakes?

Jill did not have a happy weekend and I am sure she will be pleased to see her father back home.

She made a number of mistakes in her writing. Did you notice them all? If not, correct those you missed, thinking very carefully.

18. Imran Patel Wednesday, November 24th

When I am an adult I want to be a sailer and sale round the werld. My uncle has just been stay with us. He came back from australia last week. He explaned about all the countrys he saw as he sialed out there. He did not complain at all about the time on the bote when they saw no land all.

When they arrivd in australia, the sailers all had two weeks holday. My uncle and for frends hird a car and drived into the desert. They stoped at motles hundrds of mils from anywhere for food and to sleep. He said that everyone was very friendly.

He and his frends was very sorry when they had to tern round and drive back to boat. They are quiet shore that they want to again in the futre.

18. Imran Patel Wednesday, November 24th

---

sailor sail
When I am an adult I want to be a sailer and sale round the
world. to
werld. My uncle has just been∧stay with us. He came back from
Australia explained countries
australia last week. He explaned about all the countrys he saw
sailed
as he sialed out there. He did not complain at all about the time
boat at
on the bote when they saw no land∧all.

arrived Australia, sailors
When they arrivd in australia, the sailers all had two weeks
holiday. four friends hired drove
holday. My uncle and for frends hird a car and drived into the
stopped motels hundreds miles
desert. They stoped at motles hundrds of mils from anywhere for
food and to sleep. He said that everyone was very friendly.

friends were turn
He and his frends was very sorry when they had to tern
the quite sure
round and drive back to∧boat. They are quiet shore that they
go future.
want to∧again in the futre.

Did you miss any mistakes?

Imran has exciting ideas about the future. His piece of writing is very interesting, but he did make some mistakes.

Did you notice the words in the 'a-i' family that he got wrong? If you missed any, go back and look carefully at the family.

He also has difficulties with <u>four</u> and <u>hundreds</u>. Correct the mistakes you missed, thinking very hard.

I opend the cuboard in the hall yestday to get out my dufle coat and I find it was not their.

I thort, my bother has piched it.

Mum I shoutd. Weres my duffle caot?

I don't no," said Mum. When did you last use it

Febuary, I should thinck, I said.

Haven't you seen it since" Mum asked, coming out of the kichen.

Can't rember I groned. "Quentin got it? What did he wear to school today Bet he take it.

We'll see when gets home. Wear your raicoat for now. Qick, or you'll be late for school Mum said.

"That dufle coat was a bargin, I moned as I grabed my rancoat and ran out of the front door.

19. Ria Quilter — Thursday, November 25th

opened cupboard yesterday duffle
I opend the cuboard in the hall yestday to get out my dufle

found there.
coat and I find it was not their.

thought, brother pinched
I thort, "my bother has piched it."

"Mum!" shouted. "Where's coat?"
Mum I shoutd. Weres my duffle caot?

know
"I don't no," said Mum. "When did you last use it?"

"February, think,"
Febuary, I should thinck, I said.

"Haven't you seen it since?" Mum asked, coming out of the

kitchen.
kichen.

remember," groaned. Has
"Can't rember I groned. "^Quentin got it? What did he wear to

took
school today? Bet he take it."

he raincoat Quick,
"We'll see when^gets home. Wear your raicoat for now. Qick,

or you'll be late for school," Mum said.

duffle bargain", moaned grabbed
"That dufle coat was a bargin, I moned as I grabed my

raincoat
rancoat and ran out of the front door.

Did you miss any mistakes?

Ria is certainly cross with her brother. I wonder if he really did take her duffle coat?

If you missed any of her errors, think very carefully as you correct them so that you do not make the same mistakes in your writing.

20. Kevin Rogers — Friday, November 26th

We is going to the cercus tonight. It is my brithday treat. As well the famly, for of my frend is comeing too.

This is the fist time I have been a cirkus that is not in a tent. This won is in a big round hall and there will not be any animals. I spect the clown will tirl poles, thow twnty balls up and down, then sqirt water over all of us.

You must have do a lot of traning before you can be a clown. I would be a falure, becos I canot be sure of caching won ball, let alone twnty!

20. Kevin Rogers Friday, November 26th

are circus birthday
We is going to the cercus tonight. It is my brithday treat. As
as family, four friends are coming
well ∧ the famly, for of my frend is comeing too.

first to circus
This is the fist time I have been ∧ a cirkus that is not in a tent.
one
This won is in a big round hall and there will not be any animals.
expect twirl throw twenty
I spect the clown will tirl poles, thow twnty balls up and down,
squirt
then sqirt water over all of us.

to training
You must have ∧ do a lot of traning before you can be a clown.
failure, because cannot catching one
I would be a falure, becos I canot be sure of caching won ball, let
twenty!
alone twnty!

Did you miss any mistakes?

Kevin is certainly looking forward to his birthday treat.

Like a lot of the other children in his class he finds friend a difficult word to spell. Can you spell it easily? If not look very hard at it and talk to yourself about those tricky letters i-e.

Did you notice the rest of his mistakes? If not, correct those you missed, thinking carefully.

21. Emily Smith — Monday, November 29th

My father has put a fountin into the pond in our gardn. He felt very poud, but my mother was not pleasd when the foutain squerted water her best friend.

Mum take her back into the louge to dry off but her frend souded very cross because her best skert was wet. I could see it was not a great amout of water, but Mums friend spends lot of money on clothes and is very poud of them.

She anounced, I'm not comeing to your house again until that foutain has been turnd off."

I thougt Mum was going cry. She hats to argu with people.

You can be shore I'll turn the foutain of evry time you come", she said.

The freind refusd to have a cup tea and went off home to chage her skirt. I was not sorry.

"What an orful frend," I thougt.

21. Emily Smith — Monday, November 29th

fountain garden.
My father has put a fountin into the pond in our gardn. He
proud, pleased fountain
felt very poud, but my mother was not pleasd when the foutain
squirted over
squerted water ∧ her best friend.

took lounge friend
Mum take her back into the louge to dry off but her frend
sounded skirt
souded very cross because her best skert was wet. I could see it
amount Mum's a
was not a great amout of water, but Mums friend spends ∧ lot of
proud
money on clothes and is very poud of them.

announced, coming
She anounced, "I'm not comeing to your house again until
fountain turned
that foutain has been turnd off."

thought to hates argue
I thougt Mum was going ∧ cry. She hats to argu with people.

sure fountain off every
"You can be shore I'll turn the foutain of evry time you
come", she said.

friend refused of
The freind refusd to have a cup ∧ tea and went off home to
change
chage her skirt. I was not sorry.

awful friend," thought.
"What an orful frend," I thougt.

Did you miss any mistakes?

Emily learned something about friends recently, but what about her spelling?

Did you notice the mistakes she made with words in the 'ou' family? If you missed any go and look at that word family again. Correct all of the mistakes you did not spot, thinking very carefully as you do so.

22. Will Thompson Tuesday, November 30th

It is very cold in our hous because the centrl heeting has broken down. We've all got our jeens on and thik jupers but we are still cold. The man we thougt was going to repair it has disapered and my mother cannot find another centrl heeting firm easly.

I am glad I am at school. It's nice and worm here. I feel relly sorry for my mother. It must be awful sitting in that icy cold louge. I spect she has got an ovecote on and is hopping that the heeting man will apear realy quickly.

What would the teechers do if the shool cetral heating broke down? Would they send all home?

Perhaps we would have to stay and do lessons with our ovecotes on. That is what my gradma had to do in the Secnd World War.

22. Will Thompson Tuesday, November 30th

house central heating
It is very cold in our hous because the centrl heeting has
broken jeans thick jumpers
brokn down. We've all got our jeens on and thik jupers but we
thought
are still cold. The man we thougt was going to repair it has
disappeared central heating
disapered and my mother cannot find another centrl heeting
easily.
firm easly.

warm really
I am glad I am at school. It's nice and worm here. I feel relly
sorry for my mother. It must be awful sitting in that icy cold
lounge. expect overcoat hoping
louge. I spect she has got an ovecote on and is hopping that the
heating appear really
heeting man will apear realy quickly.

teachers school central
What would the teechers do if the shool cetral heating broke
us
down? Would they send∧all home?

to
Perhaps we would have to∧stay and do lessons with our
overcoats grandma Second
ovecotes on. That is what my gradma had to do in the Secnd
World War.

Did you miss any mistakes?

Will is glad to be at school in the warm. He has made some mistakes, but he might have made more if it had been as cold at school as it is at home.

Did you spot everything? Think carefully about those you missed and then make the corrections with a coloured pencil (not red).

23. Jenny Underwood Wednesday, November 31st

We had a burglery yestday. When Mum got home in the arfternoon with the shoping, she saw that the front dor was open. She left the shoping on the step and went inside.

What a mess she saw! Curtins had been pulld down, furniter was brokn and all silver knives, fawks and spoon had disapperd. These had been weding presnts a long time ago and she was realy upset.

She went to fone the plice – and my Dad. Then she on the step otside until they arrived. Dad came first and groned when he saw the diturbance to his house. He went upstars and was even more angy with what he saw up there. His gold watch, Mum's engagment ring and the money from my saveing tin had all gone.

When he got downstars, two berly pliceman were speeking to Mum.

December 1st

23. Jenny Underwood Wednesday, November 31st

---

burglary yesterday.

We had a burglery yestday. When Mum got home in the

afternoon shopping, door

arfternoon with the shoping, she saw that the front dor was

shopping

open. She left the shoping on the step and went inside.

Curtains pulled furniture

What a mess she saw! Curtins had been pulld down, furniter

broken the forks spoons disappeared.

was brokn and all ∧ silver knives, fawks and spoon had disapperd.

wedding presents

These had been weding presnts a long time ago and she was

really

realy upset.

phone police waited

She went to fone the plice – and my Dad. Then she ∧ on the

outside groaned

step otside until they arrived. Dad came first and groned when

disturbance upstairs

he saw the diturbance to his house. He went upstars and was

angry

even more angy with what he saw up there. His gold watch,

engagement saving

Mum's engagment ring and the money from my saveing tin had

all gone.

downstairs, burly policemen speaking

When he got downstars, two berly pliceman were speeking to

Mum.

Did you miss any mistakes?

Did you notice that Jenny had forgotten how many days there are in November?

Did you spot other mistakes in this sad story? She did not get all of the 'ur' words right. Did you correct them all?

If you missed any, think very carefully about the 'tricky bits' as you make your corrections with the other coloured pencil. There were other mistakes. Think hard about these if you missed them.

24. Robert Vincent Thurday, December 2nd

I watched a football mach on telvision last nite and there was so much spawling and borling that my mother wanted to turn it off. But me and my dad was really enjoying it because our favourite teem was wining.

Then something awfull hapened. The captain of our team was injurd and we saw him spawling on the muddy ground. The firt-aid men came runing out and then he were took off on a stetcher. Later we heard he had broken his jor.

Praps my mother is right when she says that all rough play should be againt the rules.

Our team was hopless after that and the crowd stoped their borling. Dad thinks it'll be weeks before the captin is fit enough to play again.

Thursday,

24. Robert Vincent Thurday, December 2nd

---

match television night
I watched a football mach on telvision last nite and there was
sprawling bawling
so much spawling and borling that my mother wanted to turn it
were
off. But me and my dad was really enjoying it because our
team winning.
favourite teem was wining.

awful happened.
Then something awfull hapened. The captain of our team was
injured sprawling
injurd and we saw him spawling on the muddy ground. The
first-aid running was taken
firt-aid men came runing out and then he were took off on a
stretcher. jaw.
stetcher. Later we heard he had broken his jor.

Perhaps
Praps my mother is right when she says that all rough play
against
should be againt the rules.

hopeless stopped
Our team was hopless after that and the crowd stoped their
bawling. captain
borling. Dad thinks it'll be weeks before the captin is fit enough
to play again.

Did you miss any mistakes?

In his excitement about the football match, Robert forgot some of the words in the 'aw' family.

Did you spot those he got wrong? If you missed any, look at that family again and make sure you know them for your own future work.

Think carefully about all of the mistakes you missed, then correct them (not with the red pencil).

25. Gina Watson Firday, December 3rd

The school chior has been invitd to give a very important concert on telvision at Christmas. I would have been very dispointed if I had been a member.

We have to practise evry luch-time and it is quiet hard work. But the songs we're singing is good and our music teacher is fun. Enyway, It would be poitless giveing a performance on telvision if people was not going to enjoy it.

At the practice on Wenesday our music teacher said fermly, You must aviod getting a cold or sore throat. If you do, you mite lose your voise and then you would not be on telvision. So tacke car."

Friday,

25. Gina Watson — Firday, December 3rd

choir invited
The school chior has been invitd to give a very important
television
concert on telvision at Christmas. I would have been very
disappointed not
dispointed if I had ^ been a member.
every lunch-time quite
We have to practise evry luch-time and it is quiet hard work.
are
But the songs we're singing is good and our music teacher is fun.
Anyway, it pointless giving television
Enyway, It would be poitless giveing a performance on telvision
were
if people was not going to enjoy it.
Wednesday firmly,
At the practice on Wenesday our music teacher said fermly,
avoid might
"You must aviod getting a cold or sore throat. If you do, you mite
voice television. take
lose your voise and then you would not be on telvision. So tacke
care."
car."

Did you miss any mistakes?

Gina is certainly proud to be a member of the Brand's Patch school choir and will be thrilled to be on television.

She will need to learn how to spell <u>choir</u> and <u>voice</u>. Did you notice that she had these words wrong? But she did get 'to practise' right. That is very good.

Correct any mistakes you missed with your other coloured pencil (not red), thinking very carefully.

26. Max Lennox Munday, December 5th

When I am a tenager I would like to work in a supermarkit on Saterdays like my bother does now. He is forteen and really enjoys stacking grocerys on to the shelves.

Sometimes these are bargins and lot of goods has to be put in diffrent places. Its hard work but he thinks it is intresting.

Some of the grocerys come form other countrys. Chese might come from sitzerland, sasages from germany, or butter from New Zealand. the fruit and vegetables is not so easy. Potatos, tomatos and strawberries go rotten and have to be throwd away. There is always lots of choclate bars on the shelves and if your feeling hungry, it must be difficult not to take bar and have a bite. My bother wouldn't do this and neither would I. If the supmarkit boss foud out, you would get the sack.

Monday,

26. Max Lennox — Munday, December 5th

---

teenager supermarket
When I am a tenager I would like to work in a supermarkit on
Saturdays brother fourteen
Saterdays like my bother does now. He is forteen and really
groceries
enjoys stacking grocerys on to the shelves.

bargains lots have
Sometimes these are bargins and lot of goods has to be put in
different It's interesting.
diffrent places. Its hard work but he thinks it is intresting.

groceries from countries. Cheese
Some of the grocerys come form other countrys. Chese might
Switzerland, sausages Germany
come from sitzerland, sasages from germany, or butter from
The are Potatoes,
New Zealand. the fruit and vegetables is not so easy. Potatos,
tomatoes thrown
tomatos and strawberries go rotten and have to be throwd
are chocolate
away. There is always lots of choclate bars on the shelves and if
you're a
your feeling hungry, it must be difficult not to take ^ bar and
brother
have a bite. My bother wouldn't do this and neither would I. If
supermarket found
the supmarkit boss foud out, you would get the sack.

Did you miss any mistakes?

Max should learn to spell supermarket *if he wants to work in one, but he and his brother certainly sound as if they are honest boys, don't you think?*

He did make other mistakes and forgot about some important capital letters. Think carefully about any you missed and then correct them.

27. Chloe Yelton Teusday,

Yestaday my mother had take my brother to hospitel because on saterday afternoon damaged his right leg. He usully plays football with his friends on saterdays. Natrally, the boys get rough when they are playing. Boys are allways like that in football matches.

At first, Mum and Dad did take him to the docter, even though it was painful. But gradully my brother's leg began to swell. It got biger and biger, so on Monday they did take him to our docter who sent them to the hospitel.

When I got home, my brothers leg was in plarster – He had broke some litle bone. Theres no more football on Saterdays for the next few week.

Tuesday, December 6th

27. Chloe Yelton Teusday,

Yesterday to hospital
Yestaday my mother had ^ take my brother to hospitel because
Saturday he usually
on saterday afternoon ^ damaged his right leg. He usully plays
Saturdays. Naturally,
football with his friends on saterdays. Natrally, the boys get
always
rough when they are playing. Boys are allways like that in
football matches.

not doctor,
At first, Mum and Dad did ^ take him to the docter, even
gradually
though it was painful. But gradully my brother's leg began to
bigger bigger,
swell. It got biger and biger, so on Monday they did take him to
doctor hospital.
our docter who sent them to the hospitel.

brother's plaster he
When I got home, my brothers leg was in plarster – He had
broken little bones.There's Saturdays
broke some litle bone. Theres no more football on Saterdays for
weeks.
the next few week.

Did you miss any mistakes?

Chloe did not finish writing the date and did not spell <u>Tuesday</u> correctly. Did you notice? I am sure you did.

Look at mistakes you did not spot, think carefully and correct them with your other coloured pencil.

28. Paul Zoom — Wenesday, December 7

Whe I grown up I want to a pop star. Theyre usully welthy and can by lots of tresures and farst cars. I canot sing very well, but I can the guitar. If I plays it very loud and just ball out the words, some people will have lots of plesure, otlers will just get hedackes.

Ill wear jens and a lether jackit like lots of pop star do. they sometims swet as they keep juping round the stage. Its probably not a helthy way to get welthy, but that what I am goin to do.

Wednesday, 7th

28. Paul Zoom — Wenesday, December 7

When am be They're usually wealthy

Whe I ^ grown up I want to ^ a pop star. Theyre usully welthy

buy treasures fast cannot

and can by lots of tresures and farst cars. I canot sing very well,

play play bawl

but I can ^ the guitar. If I plays it very loud and just ball out the

pleasure, others

words, some people will have lots of plesure, otlers will just get

headaches.

hedackes.

I'll jeans leather jacket stars They

Ill wear jens and a lether jackit like lots of pop star do. they

sometimes sweat jumping It's

sometims swet as they keep juping round the stage. Its probably

healthy wealthy, that's going

not a helthy way to get welthy, but that what I am goin to do.

Did you miss any mistakes?

Did you miss any of Paul's mistakes? If you did, take another pencil (not red) and make the corrections.

Think very hard, so that you do not make the same mistakes yourself.

29. Mary Anderson Thurday, December 8th

All the eletric powar went of in our steet last night. their was no TV, no light and no heeting. We couldnt have eny hot drincks. Usully I have a showar befor I go to bed, but last night I had a quik cold bath with my mother hold a torch.

Then I grabed a towal, but couldnt sea weather it was mine or my brother's. I didnt put on any powdar, just jumped into my pyjama and got into bed about half sevn. It was beter than siting frezing dowstairs. Mum, Dad and my bother came up just after.

In the night, the powar came back on and as the lights flached on they waked us all up. It taked a long time to got back to sleep agin, so I feel quiet drosy this morning.

Thursday,

29. Mary Anderson Thurday, December 8th

---

electric power off street There

All the eletric powar went of in our steet last night. their was

heating. couldn't any drinks.

no TV, no light and no heeting. We couldnt have eny hot drincks.

Usually shower before

Usully I have a showar befor I go to bed, but last night I had a

quick holding

quik cold bath with my mother hold a torch.

grabbed towel, couldn't see whether

Then I grabed a towal, but couldnt sea weather it was mine or

didn't powder, jumped

my brother's. I didnt put on any powdar, just jumped into my

pyjamas at seven. better

pyjama and got into bed∧about half sevn. It was beter than

sitting freezing downstairs. brother

siting frezing dowstairs. Mum, Dad and my bother came up just

after.

power

In the night, the powar came back on and as the lights

flashed woke took get

flached on they waked us all up. It taked a long time to got back

again, quite drowsy

to sleep agin, so I feel quiet drosy this morning.

Did you miss any mistakes?

Perhaps Mary made so many mistakes because she felt drowsy. Did you spot them all? If not, think hard and take a pencil (not red) to correct them.

30. Rob Bannister — Firday, December 9th

it taked me an our to do my homwork larst nite and I rote all the rong ansers to my sums. I gess it was becos I was lisening to the TV at the same time. I ofen do that, but praps Id beter not do it wen Ive got sums for homwork

I shall feel gilty when my muther arsks to look at my book becos she allways makes me finish my homwork before I woch TV. But on Thurdays she takes my sister to Gides and my Gran comes in to look arfter me. When I sed I ofen wached TV and did my homwork at the same time, she let me do it. Mum will be cross but Im the gilty one, not Gran.

30. Rob Bannister Friday, Firday, December 9th

It took hour homework last night wrote
it taked me an our to do my homwork larst nite and I rote all

wrong answers guess because listening
the rong ansers to my sums. I gess it was becos I was lisening to

often perhaps I'd better
the TV at the same time. I ofen do that, but praps Id beter not

when I've homework.
do it wen Ive got sums for homwork

guilty mother asks
I shall feel gilty when my muther arsks to look at my book

because always homework watch
becos she allways makes me finish my homwork before I woch

Thursdays Guides
TV. But on Thurdays she takes my sister to Gides and my Gran

after said often watched
comes in to look arfter me. When I sed I ofen wached TV and did

homework
my homwork at the same time, she let me do it. Mum will be

I'm guilty
cross but Im the gilty one, not Gran.

Did you miss any mistakes?

I am glad Rob does not want his Mum to blame his Gran.

He did make a number of mistakes in this piece of writing and I am sure he was not watching television.

Did you notice them all? If not, think carefully and correct the others (not with a red pencil).

31. Jessica Clark monday, december 12th

My arnty has sed she will took my sister and me to Frarnce in the cristmas holdays. It will probly be arfter boxin Day and befor the New yere Ill have to get a parsport but my sister has allready got won becos she whent on a schol trip in the sumer. She dose french at scool so that is anuther advarntage she has.

Anty sed to me, Don't worry. my french is not good, so elizabeth can talk for us bothe. Then she give me a nise freindly smile.

Monday, December

31. Jessica Clark monday, december 12th

---

aunty said take France

My arnty has sed she will took my sister and me to Frarnce in

Christmas holidays. probably after Boxing before

the cristmas holdays. It will probly be arfter boxin Day and befor

Year. I'll passport

the New yere Ill have to get a parsport but my sister has

already one because went school summer.

allready got won becos she whent on a schol trip in the sumer.

does French school another advantage

She dose french at scool so that is anuther advarntage she has.

Aunty said "Don't My French

Anty sed to me, Don't worry. my french is not good, so

Elizabeth both". gave nice friendly

elizabeth can talk for us bothe. Then she give me a nise freindly

smile.

Did you miss any mistakes?

Did you spot the missing capital letters, as well as the spelling mistakes?

If you missed anything, think very carefully about the word family and about why you need capitals for certain words. Then take a coloured pencil (not red) and correct.

32. Ian Davies Tuseday, Dec. 13th

Uncel bill and his famly is coming to stay wiv us on fursday. there visit to England from Girmany is quiet suden. He wrote to tell us that they mite have to come back to england live. It mite be misrabel for them but wonderful four us to have our cousins to live back hear.

Thankfuly we've just had a knew bedrom bilt over the garage, so some of them will probly sleep their. It wuld be wundeful if Mum and Dad put me in the knew room with my for cousins and let Uncel bill and Arnty jane has my room.

Tuesday, December

32. Ian Davies Tuseday, Dec. 13th

Uncle Bill family are with Thursday.

Uncel bill and his famly is coming to stay wiv us on fursday.

Their Germany quite sudden.

there visit to England from Girmany is quiet suden. He wrote to

might England to might

tell us that they mite have to come back to england ^ live. It mite

miserable for

be misrabel for them but wonderful four us to have our cousins

here.

to live back hear.

Thankfully new bedroom built

Thankfuly we've just had a knew bedrom bilt over the garage,

probably there. would wonderful

so some of them will probly sleep their. It wuld be wundeful if

new four

Mum and Dad put me in the knew room with my for cousins and

Uncle Bill Aunty Jane have

let Uncel bill and Arnty jane has my room.

Did you miss any mistakes?

Ian is very thrilled about his cousins coming to stay. If he sleeps in the same room as <u>four</u> cousins, there will probably be more talking than sleep!

Look carefully at his spelling mistakes. Did you miss any? If so, think about them and mark with a coloured pencil (not red).

33. Katy England Wensday, Dec. 14th

We is probly going to Ostralia in Orgust for a holday and to sea my gradmar and grandad who live their. They went to live in perth Western Ostralia sevn years ago when I was only thee. I do rember we used to larff a lot when they were at our house. They even larffed when I was norty and this made my mother cross.

She usd to say to them,

I am your dorter and I don't want my famly to be amusd when Katy is norty. If shes norty when she gets biger you wont be pleased.

My mother told me this yesterday. Then she larffed and said, I think your gradmar and grandad will like the grown-up Katy.

I hope so!

Wednesday, December

33. Katy England Wensday, Dec. 14th

are probably Australia August holiday

We is probly going to Ostralia in Orgust for a holday and to

see grandma there.

sea my gradmar and grandad who live their. They went to live in

Perth, Australia, seven three.

perth Western Ostralia sevn years ago when I was only thee. I do

remember laugh

rember we used to larff a lot when they were at our house. They

laughed naughty

even larffed when I was norty and this made my mother cross.

used

She usd to say to them,

daughter don't family amused

"I am your dorter and I don't want my famly to be amusd

naughty. she's naughty bigger won't

when Katy is norty. If shes norty when she gets biger you wont

be pleased."

laughed

My mother told me this yesterday. Then she larffed and said,

grandma

"I think your gradmar and grandad will like the grown-up Katy."

I hope so!

Did you miss any mistakes?

Katy will have a wonderful holiday in Australia, but I think she had better really learn the 'au' family before she goes. If you missed any of her mistakes, so had you!

If you noticed them all, well done. Did you put in the speech marks as well?

34. Danny Frost Thursday, December 15th

We went on a tremendus excuson to London larst Saterday. It were my freinds birthday and his parnts arsked what he would like to do as a treat. He thort an excurson London on the trian would be marvelous.

He was alloud to take tow friends and I was won of the lucky ones. His uther friends was probly jealus.

Going on the train was great. We usally go everwhere by car and to go on the train for one and a harf ours was wondaful.

We went to see the Changing of the Gard at buckingham palace and then went to feed the pigeon in Trafalgar Sqare. after luch we Big Ben and the Houses of Parliament. Then it were time to cach the train home. We was all feeling quiet tied, but it was a marvelous day.

34. Danny Frost — Thursday, December 15th

tremendous excursion last Saturday.
We went on a tremendus excuson to London larst Saterday. It
was friend's parents asked
were my freinds birthday and his parnts arsked what he would
thought excursion to train
like to do as a treat. He thort an excurson ^ London on the trian
marvellous.
would be marvelous.

allowed two one
He was alloud to take tow friends and I was won of the lucky
other were probably jealous.
ones. His uther friends was probly jealus.

usually everywhere
Going on the train was great. We usally go everwhere by car
half hours wonderful.
and to go on the train for one and a harf ours was wondaful.

Guard Buckingham
We went to see the Changing of the Gard at buckingham
Palace pigeons Square. After
palace and then went to feed the pigeon in Trafalgar Sqare. after
lunch saw was
luch we ^ Big Ben and the Houses of Parliament. Then it were time
catch were quite tired,
to cach the train home. We was all feeling quiet tied, but it was a
marvellous
marvelous day.

Did you miss any mistakes?

Danny made quite a few mistakes, but he obviously enjoyed his visit to London with his friends.

Did you spot the errors and correct them with your red pen? If you missed any, think very hard about them and correct with a different colour.

35. Helen Goffin Friday, December 16th

This is our finel day at school befor the Cristmas holidays. We will have a concert this afternoon and I be playing a vilin solo. I onely hope it sounds allright as I a little nervus playing in front of my frends. If I do play some wrong notes they may not notis. If they do, they will probly be to plite to say anthing.

I am locking forward to Chrismas as I am hopping to have a bycycle as my present. My parnts are very silnt about it, so I am not realy sure. I will have to weight until Chrismas morning to find out.

At diner-time I must rember to take my books back to the libry and get some mor out for the holdays.

35. Helen Goffin — Friday, December 16th

final before Christmas
This is our finel day at school befor the Cristmas holidays. We

will violin
will have a concert this afternoon and I ∧ be playing a vilin solo. I

only alright am nervous
onely hope it sounds allright as I ∧ a little nervus playing in front

friends. notice.
of my frends. If I do play some wrong notes they may not notis.

probably too polite anything.
If they do, they will probly be to plite to say anthing.

looking Christmas hoping
I am locking forward to Chrismas as I am hopping to have a

bicycle parents silent
bycycle as my present. My parnts are very silnt about it, so I am

really wait Christmas
not realy sure. I will have to weight until Chrismas morning to

find out.

dinner-time remember
At diner-time I must rember to take my books back to the

library more holidays.
libry and get some mor out for the holdays.

Did you miss any mistakes?

Do you or any of your friends play a musical instrument? If so, you will understand how Helen feels before the Christmas concert.

Did you notice that she forgot the 't' in Christmas? I hope you will never forget it in your own writing. Correct the mistakes you missed, thinking carefully